STORYTIME COMPANION

Learning Games & Activities for Schools & Libraries

Carol K. Lee
and
Janet Langford

Alleyside Press
Fort Atkinson, Wisconsin

Published by Alleyside Press, an imprint of Highsmith Press LLC
Highsmith Press
W5527 Highway 106
P.O. Box 800
Fort Atkinson, Wisconsin 53538-0800

1-800-558-2110

Art: Ruth Hester. Cover Design: Frank Neu

The paper used in this publication meets the minimum requirements of American National Standard for Information Science — Permanence of Paper for Printed Library Material. ANSI/NISO Z39.48-1992.

Library of Congress Cataloging-in-Publication Data
Lee, Carol K.
  Storytime companion : learning games & activities
for schools & libraries / Carol K. Lee and Janet Langford.
    p. cm.
  Includes bibliographical references and index.
  ISBN 1-57950-019-6 (softcover : alk. paper)
  1. Reading (Early childhood) 2. Educational games.
 3. Children--Books and reading. I. Langford, Janet. II. Title.
LB1139.5.R43L44 1998
372.4--dc21   98-20793
                                      CIP

Contents

Introduction

Storytime Companion is designed to complement *57 Games to Play in the Library or Classroom*. Together they provide ideas, games and activities to support a broad and vibrant school library media program, one that addresses information literacy and literature appreciation, with links to subjects across the curriculum. *Storytime Companion* focuses on the use of literature to spark the *reading habit* for both lifelong learning and recreational reading.

Where better to create the love of reading than at the earliest level? And so, the books and activities suggested here are for the pre-school, kindergarten, and primary student. The developmental growth of the young child is an important factor in the types of activities we have provided. Students are encouraged to interact with the teacher, to work with other students, to listen, to be creative, to learn by doing, and to have fun.

The authors, a school library media specialist and a classroom teacher, have collaborated in this book to share ideas that can be used in the classroom and in the library media center. By our joint effort we hope to emphasize that the standards contained in *Goals 2000* and in *Information Literacy Standards for Student Learning* (AASL/AECT) can be reached only by the reinforcement of what is taught in both the classroom and in the library media center.

The books we have listed in this guide are suggested based on our own experience in the library and the classroom. Supplement the list with your own favorites. You may also have ideas for altering the activities or swapping the ideas from one unit with another to fit your needs.

We have not included books that were out-of-print at the time this guide was written. While we include a number of books from series built around a character or characters, we have not listed the whole series here. Our experience has been that if students have had an enjoyable encounter with a certain book character, they will surely seek out other books about that character.

Some videos, CD-ROMs, and websites are listed as reminders to tap into technology resources as well. New resources are being produced every day, and it is important to keep current to select the best of these new resources.

As in *57 Games Games to Play in the Library or Classroom*, we have provided sample game questions and patterns to make it easier to use the activities. Those who have used this book have indicated that these features have been very useful.

The introductory section, Gimmicks, is a compilation of successful techniques used to promote interest in books. These tricks of the trade serve as as a starting point from which you can build your repertoire and increase your prowess in stimulating reading interest. Expand and refine these ideas and others you may attain through "shop-talking" with other library media specialists.

Following Gimmicks are sample thematic units. Each unit begins with a suggested list of book and other resources. The books are the focal point of the storytime from which the activities emerge. We have sought to include popular titles that are likely to be available in your media center. Add other titles of your choice. Share the list and the activities with teachers who are starting to work on a particular unit.

Through the books, students learn to listen, assimilate language usage, add new vocabulary, gain insights into other cultures or lifestyles, comprehend the stories, and develop a treasure trove of stories to which they can return.

The activities that relate to these stories are purposely varied to permit their use across the curriculum. Some work better in the library media center. Some can be used in a classroom setting, during mathematics or science periods. Some are for the outdoors or in the gymnasium.

Some are to be used to introduce a unit, follow-up a story, or as part of a culmination of a unit. Literature needs to permeate the curriculum to generate and sustain the enthusiasm for books that keep the students reading.

Most of the activities provide hands-on experiences for the students. Many are designed to allow students to work as a team in small groups. We believe in the value of cooperative experiences as students learn to delegate chores, focus on individual strengths, collaborate on projects, and accept responsibility for the implementation and success of a task.

We have attempted to provide activities to promote information-seeking skills, and creativity in art, in writing, and through skits. Experiments, open-ended questions, projects, and games are included to foster thinking skills through observing, questioning, researching, and making decisions.

Some of the activities take little preparation. Others require duplicating copies for the students, gathering materials, or preparing the games, but we have sought to keep the preparation time for these activities to a minimum.

We decided to focus on fewer thematic units and present more activities rather than having many units with not as comprehensive a sampling of back-up activities. The units selected are frequently used with primary-level students.

The book concludes with a chart that identifies the recommended grade level for each of the activities and the pertinent part of the curriculum to which the skills relate.

We owe a debt of gratitude to Ruth Hester who did many of the illustrations.

# Teaching Gimmicks & Tricks

1. Create a story box.

Using the idea from *A Story, A Story* by Gail Haley (Macmillan, 1970), make a story box from an empty box. Decorate it with pictures from children's paperback club fliers or publishers' advertisements. Label it "The Story Box."

Write titles of five to ten books on cards and place them in the box. During storytime ask a student to draw a card from the box. Read the book. When the cards are gone, put another set in the box. Make sure the books are accessible.

This activity is intended to promote leisure reading, so select books that your students will enjoy. After you read a book, have it available for a limited time for students to read or browse through before returning it to the library. Remind students that they can borrow a book they really like later from the library. The books do not need to correlate to whatever units your class may be studying.

Suggested books for your story box cards

The Animal by Lorna Balian. Humbug Books, 1987. Patrick's friends are frightened by the creature they think is in his lunch bag.

The Cow Who Wouldn't Come Down by Paul Brett Johnson. Orchard, 1993. Miss Rosemary's cow ignores her pleas to come down as he cavorts in the sky.

Do Not Open by Brinton Turkle. Dutton, 1981. Miss Moody opens a strange bottle she finds on the beach and unleashes a terrifying creature.

If Everybody Did by Jo Ann Stover. Bob Jones University, 1989. Picture a whole class stepping on Daddy's toes, squeezing the cat, and making smudges on the wall.

The Long, Long Letter by Elizabeth Spurr. Hyperion, 1996. Exciting things happen to Aunt Hetta and her town with the unusual arrival of a long, long letter from her sister.

Miss Nelson Is Missing by Harry Allard. Houghton Mifflin, 1977. It's all work and no play for Miss Nelson's class when her substitute, Miss Viola Swamp, takes over.

No Jumping On the Bed! by Tedd Arnold. Dial, 1987. When Walter jumps on his bed and crashes through the floors below, others unwillingly follow.

A Story, A Story: An African Tale Retold. Retold by Gail E. Haley. Macmillan, 1970. Anansi, the spider man, buys the Sky God's stories by getting the three items the Sky God requests.

2. Take students on a make-believe trip to a distant country.

Create a pretend "suitcase" out of a legal-size folder to use with stories set in different locales.

Have your students cut out pictures of items someone might need to take on a trip (e.g. toothbrush, shampoo, clothing, etc.) or draw something they think is important to take. Keep old magazines, junk mail, and coupons to use for photos. Place the pictures in the folder. Discuss what special items a person might need to take because of the destination, such as a passport, money belt, or bottled water. See the sample geography discussion questions in Activity 3 below.

3. Read stories set in different countries or on different continents.

Keep a record of the books read by posting the titles on a large world map. Provide a simple geography lesson as a story starter.

Sample Geography Lesson

1. Using a map or globe from the library media center, locate our country.
2. Locate the setting of the story on the map or globe.
3. Locate the equator. Explain what effects being close or far away from the equator would have on the climate of the country.
4. Are there any bodies of water that need to be crossed to get from your town to that country?
5. What is the capital city?
6. What are some of the geographic features of the country? (e.g., mountains, rivers, plains, desert, bodies of water)
7. Discuss how a geographic feature would affect how people live in the country.

Sample books from around the world

AFRICA *Anansi the Spider: A Tale from the Ashanti*. Adapted by Gerald McDermott. Henry Holt, 1972. The six sons of Anansi use their unique abilities to save him.

Why Mosquitoes Buzz in People's Ears. Retold by Verna Aardema. Dial, 1975. The mosquito causes an unfortunate chain of events.

ANTARCTICA *Antarctica* by Helen Cowcher. Farrar, Straus & Giroux, 1990. The beautiful ice world of the penguins and seals is interrupted by metal enemies made by man.

Tacky the Penguin by Helen Lester. Houghton Mifflin, 1988. Hunters leave in disgust when they meet an "odd-ball" penguin.

CHINA *Tikki Tikki Tembo.* Retold by Arlene Mosel. Henry Holt, 1968. When Tikki Tikki Tembo falls into the well, his rescue is delayed because it takes so long to say his name.

Lon Po Po. Translated by Ed Young. Philomel Books, 1989. Three children outwit the wolf in this Chinese version of "Red Riding Hood."

FRANCE *Madeline* by Ludwig Bemelmans. Viking, 1967. The other children who live with Madeline in an old house in Paris now want their appendixes out so they too can get special attention.

GERMANY *The Bremen Town Musicians.* Retold by Hans Wilhelm. Scholastic, 1992. The donkey, cat, dog, and rooster, escaping the plight of old age, foil robbers.

Rumpelstiltskin. Retold by Alison Sage. Dial, 1990. Rose bargains with a little man to spin gold for her in return for her child.

ITALY *Strega Nona: An Old Tale.* Retold by Tomie de Paola. Simon & Schuster, 1975. Big Anthony cannot stop the pasta from overflowing the pot, his house, and the town.

JAPAN *The Boy of the Three-Year Nap* by Dianne Snyder. Houghton Mifflin, 1988. Lazy Taro schemes to marry a rich merchant's daughter when he sees her affluent lifestyle.

The Terrible Eek: A Japanese Tale. Retold by Patricia A. Compton. Simon & Schuster, 1991. Mishaps occur when a thief and a wolf lose their self-confidence because of something they overhear.

KOREA *Magic Spring: A Korean Folktale* by Nami Rhee. Putnam, 1993. Water from a magic spring brings happiness to an old couple and misfortune to a greedy neighbor.

MEXICO *Poppy Seeds* by Clyde R. Bulla. Puffin Books, 1994. Pablo envisions a village of beautiful flowers when he receives a gift of flower seeds.

NEW ZEALAND *The Great White Man-Eating Shark : A Cautionary Tale* by Margaret Mahy. Penguin, 1989. Norvin fools the other swimmers, including a shark, with his shark disguise.

RUSSIA *Babushka's Doll* by Patricia Polacco. Simon & Schuster, 1990. Grandmother's doll teaches Natasha a lesson in patience.

Bony-Legs by Joanna Cole. Four Winds Press, 1983. A dog and cat help Sasha escape a horrible witch who lives in a hut that stands on chicken feet.

SCANDINAVIA *Trouble With Trolls* by Jan Brett. Putnam, 1992. Treva bargains with some trolls to get back her dog.

The Mitten. Retold by Alvin Tresselt. Lothrop, Lee & Shepard, 1964. Various animals seek refuge from the bitter cold in a mitten dropped by a little boy.

UNITED STATES *The Legend of the Bluebonnet: An Old Tale of Texas.* Retold by Tomie de Paola. Putnam, 1983. She-Who-Is-Alone gives her only possession, a doll, to end a drought.

The Legend of the Indian Paintbrush. Retold by Tomie dePaola. Putnam, 1988. Paint brushes left on a hill by an artist become the Indian paintbrush flower.

VIETNAM *The Lotus Seed* by Sherry Garland. Harcourt Brace, 1993. The lotus seed, plucked by Grandmother for a special purpose, becomes a part of her family in a new country.

4. Use a prop to spark students' interest.

A prop serves as a means to introduce a book and to draw attention to storytime.

Examples

Create a floppy mop out of red yarn to wear on your head for *Mop Top* by Don Freeman. Puffin Books, 1978. Mop Top begs for a haircut when his hair is mistaken for a red mop.

Wear a top hat for *Mirette on the High Wire* by Emily A. McCully. Putnam, 1992. Mirette becomes a part of a high-wire act.

Stack several kinds of hats on your head for *Caps for Sale* by Esphyr Slobodkina. Scholastic, 1993. Monkeys steal the peddler's caps and mimic his actions.

Stuff a mitten with small plastic animals or pictures of animals for *The Mitten* by Jan Brett. Putnam, 1989; or *The Mitten* by Alvin Tresselt. Lothrop, Lee & Shepard, 1964. Animals squeeze into a mitten to escape the cold.

Show some interesting rocks for *Sylvester and the Magic Pebble* by William Steig. Simon & Schuster, 1988. Sylvester is distressed when he turns into a rock and can't undo his wish.

Wear clothing with a design that might relate to a character in the story or the plot. (e.g., teddy bears or cats)

5. Discuss the cover of the book for before reading it.

Ask students to talk about who some of the characters are and who might be the main characters. Select students to point to the title and to tell what the other words with the title mean (author or illustrator). Discuss whether the cover of the book makes them want to read it. Point out that the title usually has the larger letters.

6. Have a "guest" stop by for a visit.

The guest might be a puppet, a stuffed animal, or a pet. Tell the students the guest was invited to listen to a favorite story.

7. Use cutout pages to create a story timeline.

Cut out pages from paperback books or picture books about to be discarded. Mount them on construction paper or tagboard and laminate.

Have the students sit in a circle. Hand out completed boards to a few students. Ask who has the page with a picture from the very beginning of the story. The student shows the page. Continue in the sequence of the story.

This activity encourages students to study the illustrations and think about the sequence of events in the story.

Story line example books

The Carrot Seed by Ruth Krauss. HarperCollins, 1945. A little boy plants a carrot seed that grows even though no one in his family believed it would.

Mr. Gumpy's Outing by John Burningham. Henry Holt, 1971. The animals and children on an outing with Mr. Gumpy fall into the water when his boat tips over.

Where the Wild Things Are by Maurice Sendak. HarperCollins, 1964. A forest and "wild things" entertain naughty Max who is sent to his room without supper.

8. Compare characters, setting, and plot of similar stories.

A Venn diagram may be helpful with this activity.

Little Red Riding Hood by Lisa Campbell Ernst (Simon & Schuster, 1995) and *Red Riding Hood* by James Marshall (Dial, 1987).

Lon Po Po. Translated by Ed Young. Philomel Books, 1989.

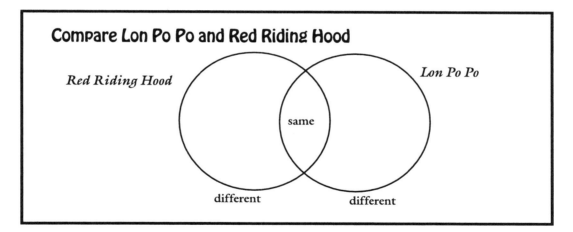

Other possible comparisons:

The Mitten by Jan Brett (Putnam, 1989) and *The Mitten* by Alvin Tresselt (Lothrop, Lee & Shepard, 1964). Animals squeeze into a mitten to escape the cold.

Three Little Pigs by James Marshall (Dial, 1989) and *True Story of the Three Little Pigs* by Jon Scieszka (Dutton, 1995).

Nanny Goat and the Seven Little Kids by Eric A Kimmel (Holiday House, 1990) and *The Wolf and the Seven Kids* by Jacob Grimm. Illus. by Bernadette Watts (North-South Books, 1995). Mother Goat saves her seven kids from the belly of the wolf.

9. Have children speculate on the story ending.

Stop reading the story just before the ending to ask the children to speculate on the ending. Compare their comments with the actual ending.

10. Make a picturebook match game.

To Make: You will need pictures of books from paperback book club fliers to create the game cards. Cut the pictures out (two of each book selected) and mount them on tagboard squares (about 4"X 4"). Laminate.

To Play: Play the game with the entire class by putting the game cards, with pictures facing down or towards the board, on a sentence or pocket chart. The students, one at a time, turn two cards over to try to create a match. Each match counts as a point. The scores may be for teams or individuals, and the game may be played with the entire class or as an independent activity with small groups or partners.

11. Keep a record of books read using marbles in a jar.

To Make: Make the jar and marbles out of construction paper (see pattern below), and display the "jar" on a bulletin board. Attach a "marble" with the author and title on it onto the jar for each book read. When the jar is full celebrate with a Read-in. Students may bring sleeping bags, snacks, and favorite books to enjoy during a work-free period.

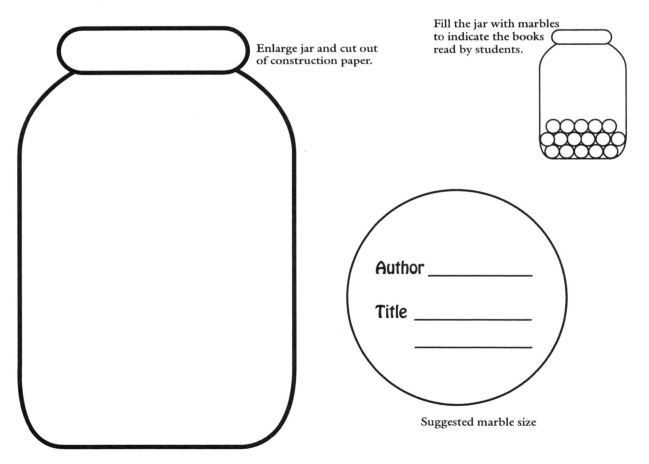

Enlarge jar and cut out of construction paper.

Fill the jar with marbles to indicate the books read by students.

Author _____

Title _____

_____

Suggested marble size

12. Create a general board game.

This game can be played as a follow-up activity at different times, depending on the questions. See the sample General Fiction Questions below. (If you are interested in general games, see *57 Games to Play in the Library or Classroom* by Carol K. Lee and Fay Edwards (also Alleyside Press) for more game ideas.)

To Make: A simple way of making the game board is to put numbers along the outer edge of a tagboard. Designate the start and end spaces. Put a bonus space for extra jumps. Stars may be used to indicate the bonus spaces. You will need a spinner, cube, or dice to determine the number of moves along the board.

To Play: Divide the class into two teams. Alternate asking questions of the team members. If the response is correct, have the player spin the spinner or toss the cube or dice. Mark the moves with clamps, clips, or clothespins. If the marker lands on a bonus space (stars), give a bonus question. If the answer is correct, move the marker to the next number.

General Fiction Questions

1. Is this a fiction or nonfiction book?
2. Find the title page.
3. Point to the title.
4. Point to the author's name.
5. Who is the illustrator?
6. What is the difference between an illustrator and an author?
7. Where is the call number?
8. What do the letters of the call number mean?
9. Does this book have an index?
10. Does this book have a table of contents?
11. Who are the characters?
12. Who are the main characters?
13. Describe the character _____.
14. Describe the setting.
15. Point to the section in the library media center where the easy fiction books are found.
16. The words _____ and _____ best describe what character?
17. Would a book written by Lorna Balian be found under the L for Lorna or the B for Balian?
18. Would a book about whales be found in the fiction section?
19. Would a book about Abraham Lincoln be found in the fiction section?
20. Would a book about Clifford be found in the fiction section?
21. Give another example of a fiction book.

13. Select stories with repetition or rhymes.

Encourage students to interact with the stories by reading titles that allow them to join in.

Books with repetition and rhymes

Brown Bear, Brown Bear, What Do You See? by Bill Martin Jr. Henry Holt, 1983. Animals are asked "What do they see?" They see other animals of different colors.

Chicka Chicka Boom Boom by Bill Martin Jr. Henry Holt, 1989. Letters of the alphabet climb up a coconut tree.

Five Little Monkeys Jumping on the Bed by Eileen Christelow. Clarion, 1989. The monkeys do not follow the doctor's orders that they should not jump on the bed.

I Know an Old Lady. Retold by Nadine Bernard Westcott. Little, Brown, 1980. Song about the consequence of an old lady swallowing a fly.

The Judge by Harve Zemach. Farrar, Straus & Giroux, 1988. The judge does not believe the warnings about the "horrible thing coming this way."

Lady with the Alligator Purse by Nadine Westcott. Little, Brown, 1988. The lady with the alligator purse prescribes pizza to Tiny Tim who ate a bar of soap.

Little Old Lady Who Was Not Afraid by Linda Williams. Harper & Row, 1986. The little old lady was not afraid of two big shoes, pants, shirt, gloves, hat, and a head that said "Boo."

The Napping House by Audrey Wood. Harcourt Brace, 1984. A child, a dog, a cat, a mouse, and a flea nap on Granny—but not for long!

14. Do an author (or illustrator) study for a week or two.

Focus on the books of a single author or illustrator. Discuss the author's life. What fact or facts would students include in a biography of the author? What factors influenced the author's work?

Compare the characters from several of the books. Are they similar or different?

Have students write a letter to the author. Send it to the author through their publisher *(if the author is still alive)*.

15. Have students make bookmarks of their favorite books or book characters.

Bookmarks should be at least 2½" wide and 8" long so there will be ample drawing space for young children. Have them use markers or crayons to decorate their pictures. Laminate the finished bookmarks.

16. Play Book Character BINGO.

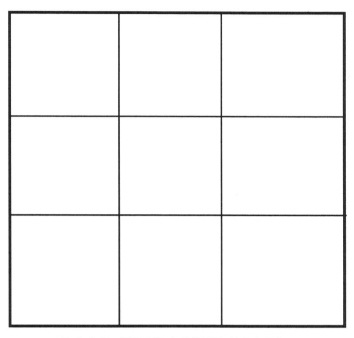

BOOK CHARACTER BINGO

Pick out nine book characters and write them in the blocks, one name per block. Please do not write them in the same order listed below.

Amelia Bedelia	Clifford	Lyle
Angus	Corduroy	Madeline
Arthur	Dragon	Miss Nelson
Babar	George (or Martha)	Peter (or Willie)
Berenstain Bears	Georgie (or the ghost)	Pig Pig
Cat in the Hat	Harry (the dirty dog)	

Use the same idea to have students create a title BINGO board. Ask the students to suggest titles of their favorite books. The students select nine titles from the list. Have students use beans to play this game or mark each corner of each block with an *X* plus the center (limited to five games). See p. 85 for a larger pattern for the BINGO board.

17. Create a browsing box using mounted book jackets.

Cut the fronts of book jackets and mount them on construction paper. Put the call number on one of the corners. Laminate the jackets. Keep the jackets in a box for the students to browse through. The students may see books that they want to borrow from the library.

18. Draw along with Harold and the Purple Crayon.

Read *Harold and the Purple Crayon* by Crockett Johnson (HarperCollins, 1983) aloud to children. As you read, have students, one at a time, come up and draw whatever Harold draws on a large sheet of newsprint *with a purple marker*. Put the picture up on the bulletin board.

19. Make dioramas of favorite scenes from story books.

Have students make dioramas of scenes from books out of shoeboxes. To make the items stand up, have students add a tab on the bottom of each picture. This is folded and taped to the bottom of the shoebox.

Shoe Box Diorama

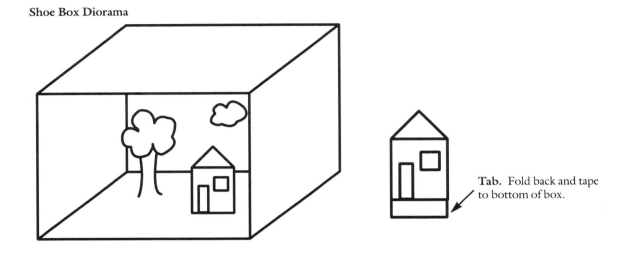

Tab. Fold back and tape to bottom of box.

20. Show a video of a story you have read.

After reading a story, you might show a video adaptation of the same story. Have the students compare the print and the nonprint versions of a story, such as:

The Day Jimmy's Boa Ate the Wash by Trinka Noble. Dial, 1980.

The Day Jimmy's Boa Ate the Wash and Other Funny Stories, 35 min. Children's Circle, 1993.

The Day Jimmy's Boa Ate the Wash, 30 min., GPN (Reading Rainbow).

Chaos results when Jimmy takes his pet snake on a field trip to a farm.

21. Celebrate Children's Book Week with a parade.

Books On Parade. Have students dress up as storybook characters. Give them the books to hold in their hands as they march. The parade may be held in the hallway, and those students not marching may sit on the floor in front of their classrooms. If you have any stuffed animals of book characters, put them on a wagon to be pulled in the parade. Decorate the wagon with balloons.

22. Invite the principal to read Thomas' Snowsuit.

The class will be amused by the principal and teacher who are frustrated and outdone by a little boy in this story by Robert Munsch (Annick Press, 1985). It will be a special treat to have it read by your school principal. You might invite other staff members, such as the custodian or the lunchroom helpers, parents, and members of the community to read to the class too. They may read a favorite book from their childhood or read a book selected by you.

Books to Use

Bear in Mind: A Book of Bear Poems. Selected by Bobbye S. Goldstein. Viking, 1989. A book of the focuses on bears through poetry.

Bears by Helen Gilks. Ticknor & Fields, 1993. Primary-level nonfiction book about bears.

The Biggest Bear by Lynd Ward. Houghton-Mifflin, 1952. Caldecott winner about a boy's dilemma when his pet bear becomes too big to manage.

Blueberries for Sal by Robert McCloskey. Puffin Books, 1976. A mix-up occurs when Sal and her mother, and a mother bear and her cub pick blueberries.

Brown Bear, Brown Bear, What Do You See? by Bill Martin, Jr. Henry Holt, 1983. Animals are asked "What do you see?" They see other animals of different colors.

Corduroy by Don Freeman. Puffin, 1988. A stuffed bear searches for his lost button, so someone will buy him.

Jesse Bear, What Will You Wear? by Nancy W. Carlstrom. Simon & Schuster, 1994. Jesse Bear wears pants that dance, a rose on his toes, and sand on his hand, among other things.

A Mother for Choco by Keiko Kasza. Putnam, 1992. Choco discovers what a mother is all about — kindness, understanding, and love.

A Pocket for Corduroy by Don Freeman. Puffin, 1993. In this second Corduroy book, the stuffed bear searches for a pocket in a coin laundry.

Teddy Bear, Teddy Bear: A Classic Action Rhyme. Illustrated by Michael Hague. Morrow, 1993. This is an illustrated version of a popular nursery rhyme for toddlers.

Tops & Bottoms. Adapted by Janet Stevens. Harcourt Brace, 1995. By outwitting Lazy Bear, Hare manages to feed his hungry family.

We're Going On a Bear Hunt retold Michael Rosen. Simon & Schuster, 1989. Many a child has gone on this bear hunt using their hands as feet.

Other Media

Corduroy. 38 min. Children's Circle, 1993. (videocassette)

Corduroy and Other Stories. 16 min. Weston Woods, 1984. (videocassette)

Mammals. National Geographic Society, 1993. (CD-ROM) "Bears." Information on size, habitat, location, and food.

1. Tell Me

Start the unit on bears by having students tell you what they know about bears. Record their statements on chart paper. Put the chart paper away until the end of the unit. At the culmination of the unit, show your students the chart. Have them tell you if they were wrong about any previous information or if they have any new information to add. Add the information with a different-colored marker so students can see how much they have learned about bears.

2. Bear Rubbing

By making a rubbing of a bear's paw, students can compare the size of the bear's foot with their own feet. Directions for the rubbing are provided on the next page. (Instead of using the tagboard, you can also make a rubbing by using glue to outline the bear's paw. When the glue hardens, continue with the rest of the directions.) This is a good activity to follow-up *We're Going On a Bear Hunt*. Discuss how you can tell if a bear is near.

3. Locating Information About Bears

Demonstrate how icons are used in a CD-ROM to locate certain information. Ask the students what information would the icons for camera, globe, ruler, and pages in the National Geographic CD-ROM *Mammals* give them. Have them tell you how to search for information about bears. Follow their directions and hunt through trial and error.

4. Brown Bear, Brown Bear

Follow-up reading *Brown Bear, Brown Bear* with a writing activity. Have students make their own new sentences by changing the names of the animals and using different adjectives or colors.

Examples:

I see a black seal looking at me.

I see a silly rhino looking at me.

Put photographs of students on the bulletin board. Have students write "I see _____ looking at me. Baby pictures would be great fun.

5. Comparing Characters

After reading *Blueberries for Sal* use the Venn diagram on p. 20 to have students compare the characters of Sal and Little Bear. You can also do this activity with other characters such as Choco and the bear in *A Mother for Choco.*

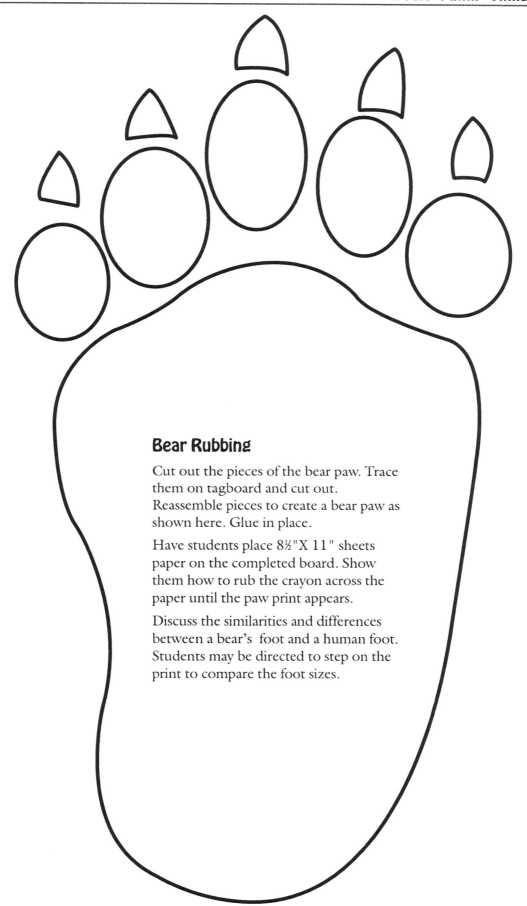

Bear Rubbing

Cut out the pieces of the bear paw. Trace them on tagboard and cut out. Reassemble pieces to create a bear paw as shown here. Glue in place.

Have students place 8½"X 11" sheets paper on the completed board. Show them how to rub the crayon across the paper until the paw print appears.

Discuss the similarities and differences between a bear's foot and a human foot. Students may be directed to step on the print to compare the foot sizes.

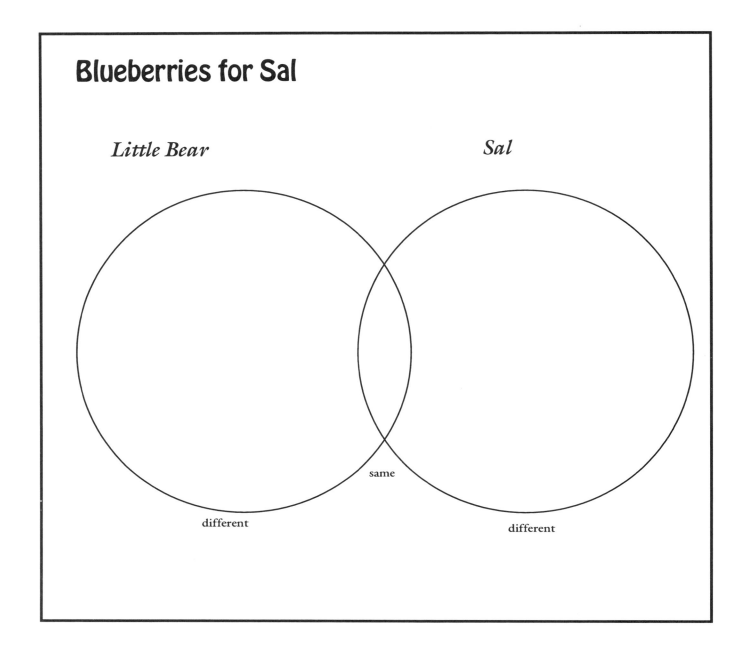

Blueberries for Sal

Little Bear   *Sal*

same

different   different

likes blueberries   gets lost
furry   helps can berries
carries pail   girl
clothes   cub
paws   eats berries
follows mother   growls

Venn Diagram comparing characters in *Blueberries for Sal*. (Activity 5, p. 18.)

6. Fish for the Bears

To Make: Prepare for this activity by cutting about twenty fish out of construction paper. Write a statement about bears on each fish.

To Play: Divide the class into two or more teams. The object is to catch fish for each team's bear. Each team player gets to bring home a fish by correctly answering a question about bears. Direct the students to answer true or false. If the student answers correctly, give that fish to the team. If the response is incorrect, the fish "got away." The side with the most fish wins the game.

The following are examples of statements to use with kindergarten or primary-level students:

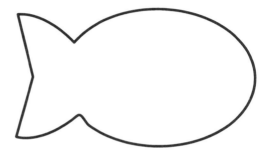

1. Bears eat other animals. *(true)*
2. Bears make good pets. *(false)*
3. Bears are mammals. *(true)*
4. Bears have bones. *(true)*
5. Bears have fins. *(false)*
6. A kitten is a baby bear. *(false)*
7. All bears have brown fur. *(false)*
8. All bears are dangerous. *(true)*
9. Bears have five toes on each foot. *(true)*
10. Bears have claws in their mouth. *(false)*
11. Polar bears can be found in _____ (your state). *(false)*   If Alaska: *(true)*
12. The hind legs of a bear are the front legs. *(false)*
13. Grizzly bears are too big to run. *(false)*
14. Eskimos eat polar bears and use their fur. *(true)*
15. A bear's home is called a den. *(true)*
16. Most bear cubs are born in the winter. *(true)*
17. Besides meat, bears like berries, fruits, and nuts. *(true)*
18. A book like *Corduroy* is a fiction book. *(true)*
19. The name of a book like *The Biggest Bear* is called the author. *(false)*
20. The illustrator for *The Biggest Bear* won the Caldecott Award. The illustrator is the writer. *(false)*
21. The title is found on the spine of the book. *(true)*

7. A Pocket for Corduroy

Show the students how to fold a paper pocket (origami) as a follow-up activity to *A Pocket for Corduroy* and *Corduroy*. Cut 8" squares out of copier paper. Have students fold according to the directions on the next page. Play hide and seek with a cardboard button. A regular button will be too thick to be hidden in the paper pockets.

Discuss corduroy (cloth) by having samples of corduroy and other fabrics for students to feel and compare. Talk about the texture of different types of materials used to make clothing. Examples: silk, wool, flannel, leather, rayon, denim, and cotton.

A Pocket for Corduroy

Follow the directions below to make a pocket for Corduroy. Then draw a button on a small card. Select a child to slip the button (while all eyes are closed) in one of their pockets. Have children guess whose pocket has the button. The student with the button doesn't try to guess during that hunt.

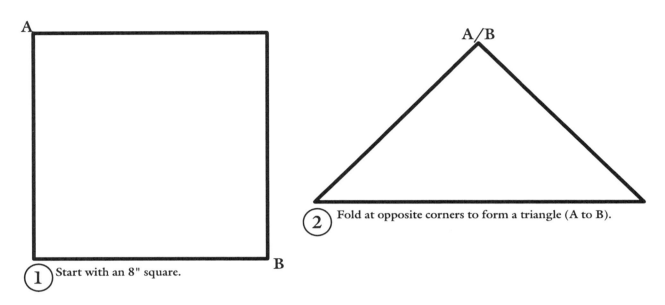

(1) Start with an 8" square.

(2) Fold at opposite corners to form a triangle (A to B).

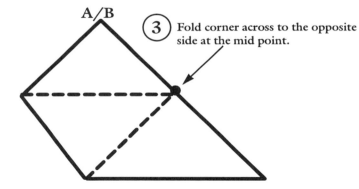

(3) Fold corner across to the opposite side at the mid point.

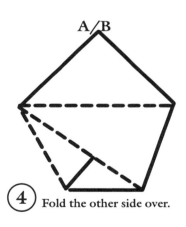

(4) Fold the other side over.

(6) Open the pocket.

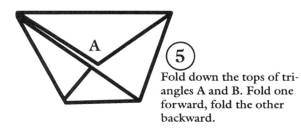

(5) Fold down the tops of triangles A and B. Fold one forward, fold the other backward.

8. Stuffed Bears

Divide the class into groups of four students. Have each group use the opaque projector to trace a bear. Select a different bear for each group and have them put two sheets of paper together so they can cut two bears at once. After the bears are cut, staple the two bears together, leaving an opening, and have the students color the bears. Stuff the bears with crumpled newspapers and staple the opening.

Place the bears around the room and outside the classroom door. Put a sign up that says

BEWARE OF THE BEARS!

9. Sponge Bear/Number Book

Make a sponge bear for students to use as a printing stamp. Have students dip the bear in brown paint and dab on paper. They may add facial features and clothing using markers.

Pattern for sponge bear

Have them make a class book using pages created with the sponge bears. Write the numbers 1– 10 on ten separate pages, one number per page. You might want to do two sets so each student will have a page. Assign a number to each child. Have children stamp the number of bears that corresponds to their number on their assigned page. For the higher numbers, have the students with the lowest numbers help decorate the bears. Bind the books to keep in the room for the students to enjoy.

10. Bear Contest

Provide your students, especially the ones who like to draw, with an opportunity to be creative. Duplicate the Bear Contest sheet on the next page for each child. Have students select a contest category in which to enter their bear. They may use markers, crayons, or colored pencils to decorate the bears.

Ask other adults from your school's staff to judge the winners of the various categories. Put the winning pictures up on the bulletin board. Place blue ribbons on each picture. Use with *Jesse Bear, What Will You Wear?*

Bear Contest

NAME _____   CHOICE _____

1. Silly Bear   4. Space Bear
2. Scary Bear   5. Best-Dressed Bear
3. Rock Bear   6. Sports Bear

11. Pop-Up Bear

After reading **_Bear in Mind_**, have students make a Pop-Up Bear to display their own work on bears. Have students do a simple writing activity such as thinking of words pertinent to bears that begin with the letters *B, E, A,* and *R*. They may do other writing tasks depending on their abilities.

To make the bear, duplicate the pattern on the next page and have the students complete the bear's face with crayons or colored pencils. Follow the directions below for cutting and folding the bears. Children will need help with the folding.

Have students print their completed BEAR writings inside the folder under the pop-up bear.

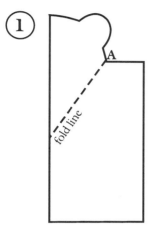

Copy pattern onto 8½" X 11 sheet. Fold in half.

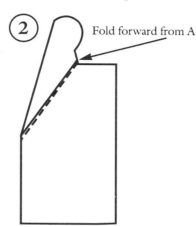

Fold forward from A

Fold to 1" below the bear's chin.

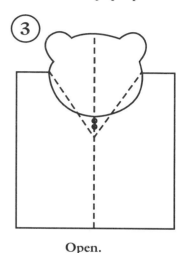

Open.

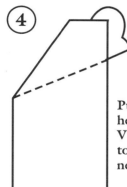

Push from back of bear's head and fold, using the V lines and the center line to naturally create the next fold.

(5) Create folders from a separate sheet of construction paper folded in half. Paste the pop-up bear inside the folder so it pops up when folder is opened.

Have students decorate folders.

12. Big, Bigger, Biggest Bear

Follow-up **_The Biggest Bear_** by having students measure bears with rulers. Duplicate the two sample pages (pp. 27–28) for each student. Have them cut out the bears on the dotted lines and then them. Direct them to place the bears in order according to size (smallest to largest; largest to smallest).

Ask them the size of the fifth bear; the size of the second bear; etc. Have them line the bears in any order. Ask individual students to tell who was first, last, fourth, etc.

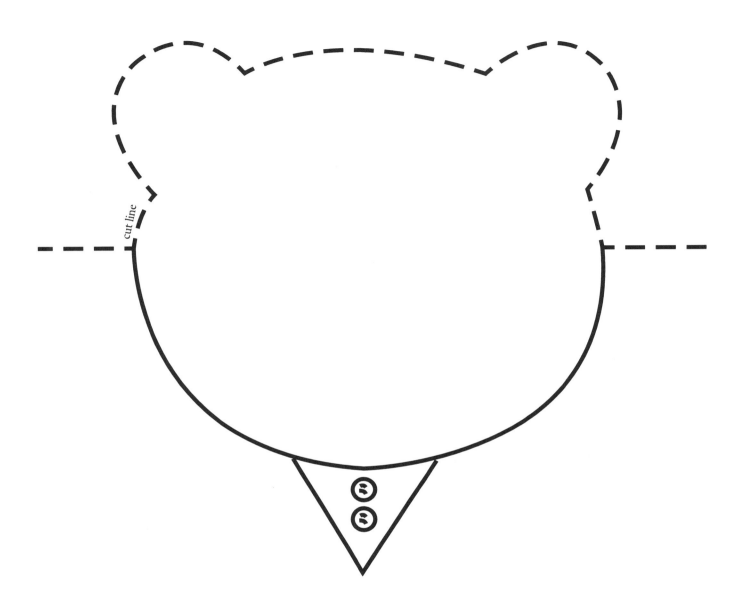

cut line

inches

Big, Bigger, Biggest Bear Directions

Cut the five bears out on the dotted lines. Use a ruler to measure how tall each bear is in inches.

Then put the bears in order from smallest to largest.

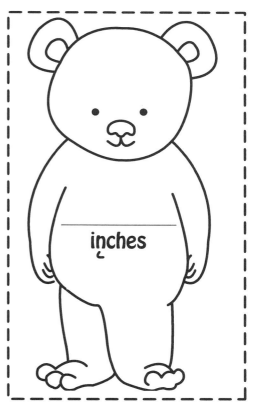

inches

13. Bear Puppet

Teach the *Teddy Bear, Teddy Bear* rhyme. Have children say the rhyme with a bear puppet made out of a paper bag. See the pattern for the paper-bag bear puppet on p. 30. Students can also act out the rhyme without a puppet.

14. My Favorite Bear Story

Ask the students what was their favorite bear story. Usse the sample graph page (p. 31) to graph student responses. Record their votes, one vote per child, by coloring the appropriate number of squares.

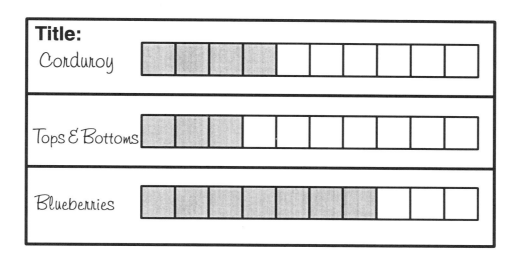

15. Bear Day

Have children bring their teddy bears to school as a culminating activity on this unit. The students can share stories about their bears. Plan to have extra bears for those students who forget or those who don't have bears.

Show a video about a bear character, such as ***Corduroy and Other Stories***. Have some treats with honey (honey and biscuit) or blueberries (***Blueberries for Sal***).

face

body

Enlarge and color the two pieces of the bear puppet. Cut out. Paste the face and body on a paper bag (lunch-bag size) as shown.

What Is Your Favorite Bear Story?

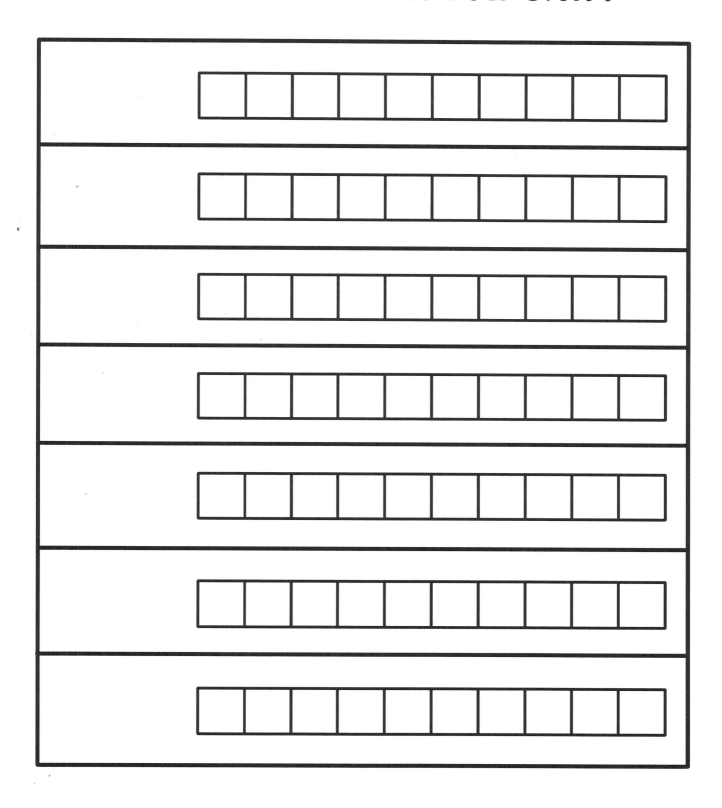

 Fish Funtasy

Books to Use

Big Al by Andrew Clements. Simon & Schuster, 1988. No one wants to be friends with a fish as ugly and scary as Big Al until he rescues them.

Fish Is Fish by Leo Lionni. Pantheon Books, 1970. A fish wants to see the world that his friend frog describes.

Fish Out of Water by Helen Palmer. Beginner Books, 1961. Problems occur when Otto eats himself out of his fish bowl.

The Great White Man-Eating Shark: A Cautionary Tale by Margaret Mahy. Penguin, 1989. Norvin fools the other swimmers, including a shark, with his shark disguise.

Harry By the Sea by Gene Zion. HarperCollins, 1965. Harry is mistaken for a sea monster when he gets covered with seaweed.

McElligott's Pool by Dr. Seuss. Random House, 1974. You never know what you might catch in McElligott's pool.

One Fish Two Fish Red Fish Blue Fish by Dr. Seuss. Random House, 1966. Dr. Seuss starts this book with an assortment of fish and branches off to other zany characters.

Rainbow Fish by Marcus Pfister. North-South Books, 1992. Rainbow Fish learns that selfishness leads to loneliness.

Swimmy by Leo Lionni. Pantheon Books, 1963. Swimmy teaches the little fish to swim in a group.

Other Media

Great White Man-Eating Shark. 10 min. Weston Woods, 1991 (videocassette)

Louis the Fish. 30 min. GPN (videocassette) *Reading Rainbow* features Arthur Yorink's book about a butcher who becomes a fish.

One Fish Two Fish Red Fish Blue Fish. 30 min. Random House, 1989.

Websites

Ocean of Know: Sharks <http://www.oceanofk.org/sharks/sharks.html/>

Sea World <http://www.seaworld.org>

Oregon Coast Aquarium <http:www.aquarium.org/home.html>

1. Fun With Goldfish

Use goldfish to have students do simple math problems. Give each student ten goldfish crackers to place on the ocean scene as you tell a story. The sample ocean scene follows this page.

Sample stories:

Three fish swim into a cave. Two fish come swimming by. They are startled when they see a huge, hungry shark headed their way. They quickly hide in the seaweed. Three fish are swimming together, looking for food. They try to go into the cave. It is too crowded in there. So one swims to the top and one searches for food on the ocean floor. Two fish pass by and swim away. How many are still in the cave? How many fish are in the ocean scene?

Two goldfish went out for a swim. They called three friends to come out to play. Now how many are swimming in a school? $2 + 3 = 5$. Eight fish were swimming past the cave. A huge octopus swooped out of the cave and frightened two away. How many of the 8 were left? Write the problem: $8 - 2 = 6$

Have students take turns telling goldfish stories. After the doing this activity, the students may eat the crackers.

2. Swimmy and Friends

Introduce *Swimmy* by having a goldfish swim around the room. Place a goldfish in a glass dish with water. Put the dish on an overhead projector. Turn the projector on and direct the students to imagine this fish swimming in a big ocean. Do not leave the lights on for very long as the water will get warm.

As a follow-up activity to *Swimmy*, give students about fifteen goldfish crackers. Have them draw the outline of a fish using the crackers.

3. Class Book

Have students make a class book after reading *One Fish Two Fish Red Fish Blue Fish*. Each student will be responsible for illustrating one page with unusual fish. Collect the pages and bind them together to keep in the classroom for all to enjoy.

4. Class Pool

Follow-up reading *McElligott's Pool* by having students create their own fantastic fish. Have them cut out the fish and put them on a bulletin board with the caption:

M___ (Mr. Mrs. Ms.) _____'S POOL.

5. Lap Chalkboard Quiz

Divide the class into groups of four to five students. Give each group a lap chalkboard (sometimes called chalkboard slate), chalk, and eraser. Designate the recorder for each team. Have them look for information about fish in one or more resources. Ask questions related to the sea. See the examples on the p. 35.

The teams decide on the answer by group consensus. The recorder writes the answer, either a letter or yes or no.

Direct the recorders to hold up the answers at the command, "Boards Up!" Give each team that has the correct answer a point. Then direct them with a "Boards Down. Erase!" command. The recorder is the only one to write and erase the team's answers.

Continue until all questions have been asked. Count the scores and announce the results.

Reminder: Give multiple choice questions or questions that require minimum writing as the space on the board is limited.

Sample Questions

1. Yes or no? Fins help the fish to move. *(yes)*
2. Yes or no? Most fish have only one fin. *(no)*
3. Gills help fish …
   a. eat   b. breathe   c. catch other fish   *(b)*
4. The bodies of most fish are covered with
   a. scales   b. fur   c. shells   *(a)*
5. Yes or no? Baby fish are hatched from eggs. *(yes)*
6. How many arms does an octopus have? *(8)*
7. Is a whale a fish? *(no)*
8. Is a shark a fish? *(yes)*
9. An octopus doesn't have which one of these?
   a. eyes   b. poison   c. bones   *(c)*
10. Which fish looks like a snake?
    a. jellyfish   b. eel   c. lobster   *(b)*
11. Yes or no? Is a crab a fish? *(no)*
12. Which animal does not have a shell?
    a. lobster   b. turtle   c. jellyfish   *(c)*
13. Yes or no? Most fish do not have teeth. *(no)*
14. Yes or no? Dolphins are fish. *(no)*
15. Which ocean borders our country?
    a. Indian Ocean   b. Antarctic Ocean   c. Pacific Ocean   *(c)*

6. Sea Puzzle

Use the sample ocean scene page (p. 34) to have students make puzzles to share. Direct them to add more sea animals to the scene and to color the picture. Paste each page onto tagboard making sure all areas have glue on them. Laminate their pictures. Have them cut the pictures into puzzle pieces and put them into plastic sandwich bags, one set per bag.

Have the students exchange bags and put puzzles together made by their classmates.

7. Fishing for Words

To Make: Duplicate the pictures of sea animals on pp. 37–38. Color and cut out about 25 animals, laminate, and attach brads or paper clips to them. Use a water soluble marker to write words on the cutouts related to sea animals. Tie a magnet to a string and tie the string to a long stick or a yardstick. Put the animals in a cardboard box. For older children, have them search for the meaning of several of the words in the library's dictionary.

Sample Words

gill	water	shark	squid
fin	salt	crab	dolphin
eel	whale	fish	mammal
sea	ocean	turtle	octopus
porpoise	jellyfish	school	seashell
seal	gull	walrus	ray

To Play: Divide the class into two teams. Give each student a turn to come up to "fish." When that student catches a fish, read the word on the fish for first-letter identification or show the word and have the student read the word.

If the student can correctly identify the beginning letter of the word or can read the word, his/her team claims that catch. If not, the fish "got away" and is put back into the box. At the end of the period, count the catch (one point per animal). You can designate more than one point for the difficult words. The team with the most points wins the game.

8. Rainbow Fish

Follow up reading *Rainbow Fish* by having students decorate a fish with crayon and sequins.

Discuss sharing. Have students compare *Rainbow Fish* at the beginning of the story and at the end of the story.

9. Three-Dimensional Fish

Duplicate the 3-D fish on the next page for each student. Have each child color his or her fish. Then have students write a word on each of the four corners, one word per corner, that pertains to the fish. On the upper-right side of the diamond shape, have students write an adjective. Have them write a noun on the bottom right, a verb on the bottom left, and an adverb on the top left side of the diamond. This is to give students practice in using words from the different parts of speech.

1 Fold paper in half. The fold should divide the fish into left and right sides. Then cut along the dotted line.

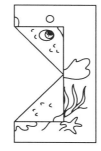

2 Fold edges back from the cut line along the edges of the fish head.

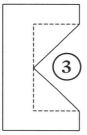

3 Open the paper. Reverse the first fold to close the booklet with the fish face inside. As you close the paper, push the top part of the fish's face upward and the bottom part downward. Crease the paper.

4 Paste the outside of the paper to the inside of a folded piece of construction paper. When the booklet is opened, the fish's mouth will pucker out. Have students decorate the cover (outside) of their booklets.

10. Fish Mobile

Duplicate the sample fish below for each student. Cut and paste it on tagboard or copy onto tagboard and cut out. Cut squares out of colorful tissue paper. Make a wash of one part glue and two parts water.

Have students brush the fish with glue mixture and place tissue squares on the glue. Brush again with the glue. Wait for the picture to dry. Have students make fish eyes out of wiggly craft eyes or out of sequins, rhinestone, or pom-poms. Punch a hole on top of the fish for hanging.

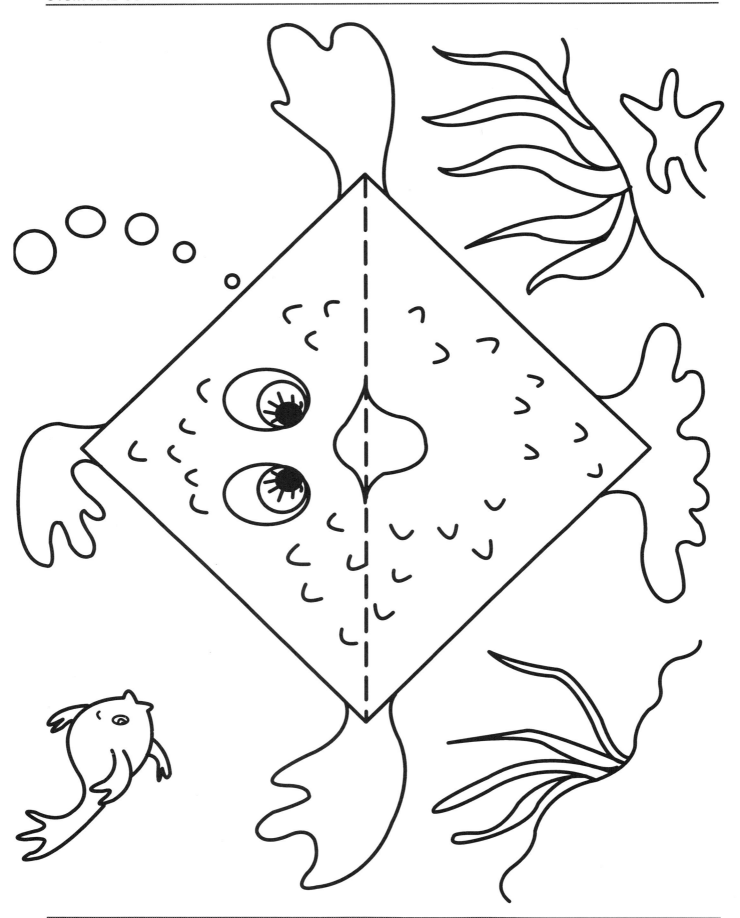

11. Fish Treat

Prepare "berry blue" gelatin as directed on the package. Pour about three inches of gelatin mix into individual small clear plastic cups for each student. When the gelatin begins to congeal, put a couple of gummi fish in each cup. You can get the gummi fish from a grocery store. Have students eat this gelatin dessert as a culminating activity on the unit on fish.

12. Sea Animals - Sources of Information

Divide the class into groups of four or five students. Duplicate Sea Animals – Sources of Information and give it to the groups to hunt down information from the sources indicated.

The purpose of this activity is give the students practice in searching for information from the various resources. The students do not need to report on their topic. They will report on where they could get information on their topic.

Assign several sea animals so that each team member will have experience in searching for a topic from more than one resource.

13. I Was There!

Follow-up *The Great White Man-Eating Shark* by having students pretend to be at the beach while on vacation in New Zealand. Direct them to send a postcard to a classmate telling of how they reacted to Norvin's trickery.

This will be a good opportunity to continue sharing sources of information with the students — in this case, about New Zealand. Have them tell you how to locate a nonfiction book on New Zealand using the computer catalog, this book, and information on the CD-ROM programs. Also have them tell you how to find information in the reference books.

TO:

Draw a scene from New Zealand on the back.

Nonfiction Book

Title _____

Author's name _____

Call number _____

Fiction Book

Title _____

Author's name _____

Call number _____

Periodical

Title of periodical _____

Title of article _____

Date of periodical _____

Page number _____

Reference Book

Title of book _____

Volume number _____

Page number _____

CD-ROM

Title of CD _____

Subject _____

4 Little Critter Books

Books to Use

Anansi the Spider. Adapted by Gerald McDermott. Henry Holt, 1972. The six sons of Anansi use their unique abilities to save him.

The Bee Tree by Patricia Polacco. Philomel, 1993. When Grandpa lets a bee out of a jar, Mary Ellen and others pursue it in search of the bee tree.

I Know an Old Lady. Illustrated by Glen Rounds. Holiday House, 1990 or
I Know an Old Lady. Retold by Nadine Bernard Westcott. Little, Brown, 1980. Song about the consequence of an old lady who swallowed a fly.

Inch by Inch by Leo Lionni. Mulberry Books, 1960. An inchworm escapes being eaten by obliging and outwitting the birds.

Two Bad Ants by Chris Van Allsburg. Houghton Mifflin, 1988. Two wayward ants decide to return to the safety of their ant colony after some harrowing experiences.

The Very Busy Spider by Eric Carle. Philomel Books, 1984. The spider is too busy spinning his web to join the other animals who invite him to do things with them.

The Grouchy Ladybug by Eric Carle. HarperCollins, 1977. Each time the grouchy ladybug challenges others to fight, it is she who backs off.

The Very Hungry Caterpillar by Eric Carle. Philomel Books, 1969. A week of eating fruits and snacks ends with the caterpillar settling into a cocoon.

The Very Lonely Firefly by Eric Carle. Philomel Books, 1995. A firefly discovers many different kinds of lights as he searches for other fireflies.

The Very Quiet Cricket by Eric Carle. Philomel Books, 1990. A cricket tries very hard to return the greetings of other animals but remains silent until he finally learns to chirp.

Why Mosquitoes Buzz in People's Ears. Retold by Verna Aardema. Dial Books, 1975. The mosquito causes an unfortunate chain of events.

Other Media

Bugs. 30 min. GPN. (videocassette) LeVar Burton hunts for monarch butterflies in Mexico and visits an insect zoo.

Spiders. 30 min. Eastman Kodak Company, 1988. Shows how spiders create webs. (videocassette)

The Very Hungry Caterpillar. 30 min. Scholastic Productions, 1995. (videocassette)

Welcome to the Wonderful of Insects. "The Spiders."
<http: //www.ex.uc.uk/~gjlramel/six.html> (website)

1. Inch by Inch

Follow-up reading *Inch by Inch* by having students measure with inch worms. Cut out about 50 inchworms. Divide the class into small groups or partners. Give each group about ten inchworms. Have them measure objects in the room, record their measurements, and report to the entire group. Students may use inchworms in any way they wish to do the measuring, e.g., side-by-side or just one like a ruler. Students may also be asked to predict how many inches an object will be. Examples of objects to measure: pencils, crayons, markers, erasers.

Inchworm pattern: Put two additional papers underneath original so you can cut three at a time.

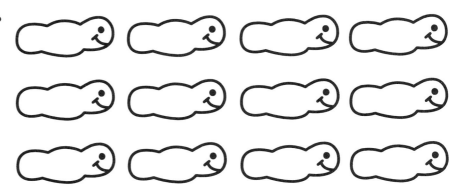

2. Who's Missing?

Play this game after reading *The Grouchy Ladybug*. Prepare for the game by cutting out the nine ladybugs on the next page. Put eight on a tray. Give your students a few seconds to see the ladybugs. Cover tray with a cover sheet. Ask the students which ladybug is missing. Continue by switching the missing ladybug, giving each student a chance to answer.

3. Who Is Grouchy?

Follow up reading *The Grouchy Ladybug* by having students make grouchy faces. Continue by having them make facial expressions of excitement, surprise, fear, pleasure, disgust, sadness, and pain. Select different students to show their faces.

4. The Very Awesome Caterpillar

Read *The Very Hungry Caterpillar.* Divide the class into two teams. Draw two caterpillar faces on the board as shown:

Team 1   Team 2

Alternate asking each team questions related to caterpillars and butterflies. Accept answers from volunteers from the groups rather than answers decided by consensus of the group. If a player correctly answers a question, add a segment to the caterpillar as shown. The caterpillar with the most segments is declared the most awesome caterpillar.

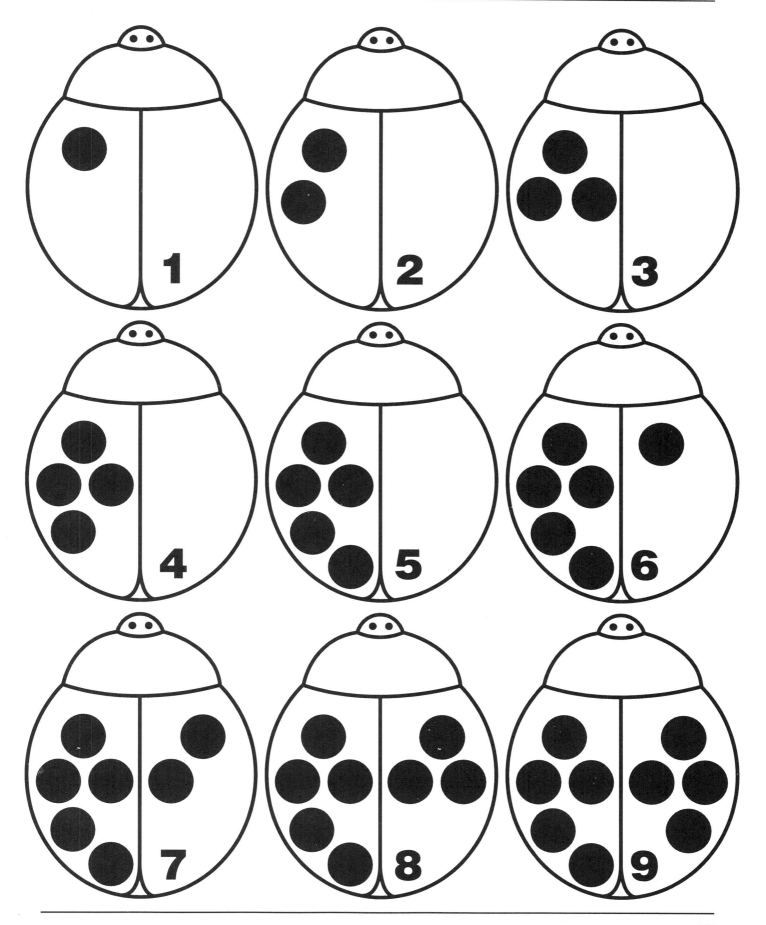

The Very Awesome Caterpillar Sample Questions

1. Is *The Very Hungry Caterpillar* a fiction or nonfiction book? *(fiction)*
2. Is Eric Carle the author or the title? *(author)*
3. Locate the call number. [Give book to student] *(on the spine)*
4. Locate the title. [Give book to student] *(on the cover, spine, or title page)*
5. A true book about caterpillars is called a _____ book. *(nonfiction)*
6. True or false? Caterpillars are hatched from eggs. *(true)*
7. Who is a character in *The Very Hungry Caterpillar*? *(caterpillar)*
8. True or false? All caterpillars are green. *(false)*
9. Why does the caterpillar shed its skin. *(As it grows, the skin gets tight)*
10. The caterpillar uses its silk thread to build a house. The house is called a
    a. nest   b. larva   c. cocoon   *(c)*
11. Who lays the eggs — the butterfly or the caterpillar? *(butterfly)*
12. What do caterpillars eat? *(leaves, fruits, vegetables)*
13. True or false? Butterflies are insects. *(true)*
14. Where do butterflies find the nectar they eat? *(flowers)*
15. Give one reason caterpillars are useful to people. *(silk)*
16. Give one reason caterpillars may be harmful to people *(eat plants, crops)*

5. Critter Hunt

Duplicate the sheet of sample leaves on the next page. Cut out at least ten leaves. You can color the maple and oak leaves with different colors to add more leaves. Laminate. You can use the sample inchworm from Inch by Inch (Activity 1, p. 44) for this activity. Lay the leaves flat on a table or tray. Hide the worm or a picture of another bug under one of the leaves. Have students hunt for the worm by selecting a leaf to look under.

6. Parts of an Insect

Divide the class into two groups. Direct the students to determine as a group where to place themselves, standing up or sitting, to show the various parts of an insect's body. They should include the head, thorax, abdomen, two antennae, six legs, and wings. Have them visit the school library media center to locate pictures of different insects so they can see the similarities and differences.

7. Parts of an Insect – Songs

Head Thorax Abdomen

(Sing to the tune of "Head, Shoulders, Knees, and Toes.")

Head, thorax, abdomen, abdomen (use both hands to touch head, chest, abdomen)
Head, thorax, abdomen, abdomen
Oh, add six legs and two antennae (arms out and wave hands up and down for the six legs; point fingers from head for the antennae)
Head, thorax, abdomen, abdomen

The students will build themselves into an insect.

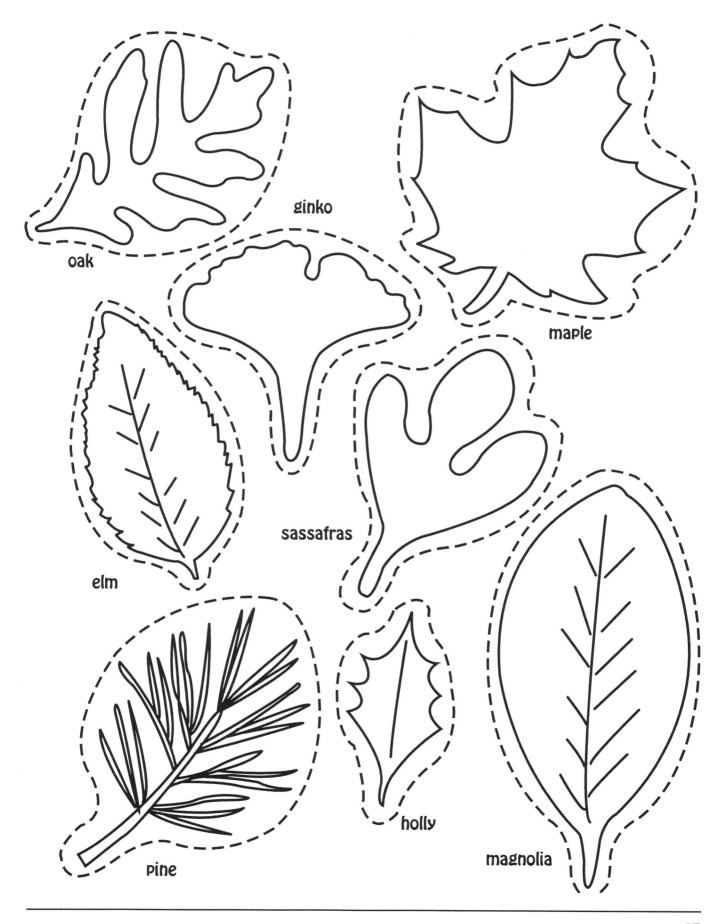

oak

ginko

maple

elm

sassafras

pine

holly

magnolia

Hey, Ho the Buggy-O
(Sing to the tune of the "Farmer In The Dell")
Choose one student to start as the head.

Oh, the head picks a thorax, the head picks a thorax,
Hey, ho the buggy-o, the head picks a thorax

(Student skips to pick a child and kneels down with head down)

The thorax picks an abdomen, the thorax picks an abdomen,......

The abdomen picks a leg, ...(Continue until six legs are picked)

The leg picks an antenna, ...

Now we've made a bug, now we've made a bug, ...
Hey, ho the buggy-o, now we've made a bug.

Each time a student picks another student, that student squats down at the appropriate place to continue building the insect.

8. Caterpillar Treat

Get miniature marshmallows, marshmallow creme, and chocolate Graham crackers. Have students dab creme on marshmallow as with glue and place on the cracker squares. Line up at least four marshmallows to look like a caterpillar. Decorate caterpillar with candy decorator beads and use creme to make the sprinkles adhere to the caterpillar. You can use licorice for the antennae and add green food color to the creme.

9. Buggy Thumbprints

Have students create bugs from their thumbprints for bookmarks or for number books. Use stamp pads with colorful ink. Share Ed Emberley's thumbprint books with them just to give them some idea of how to decorate the thumbprints. Do not let them copy from the books.

10. Praying Mantis Tag

Play this game in a gymnasium or on the playground. Have students stand in a line, side by side. Mark a "safe" line or finish line on the opposite side. The teacher is the praying mantis, and the students are the grasshoppers. The teacher says, "Be careful little grasshoppers, I may eat you!" When the teacher says "eat you!" the students run to the "safe" line. If she touches a student, the student gets to be a praying mantis, too. The game continues until all grasshoppers turn into praying mantises.

11. Bookworm Pal

Have students decorate old ties using a glue gun, scraps of cloth, beads, and sequins. They may wear their ties at the culmination of the bug unit or during special times such as Children's Book Week and I Love to Read Week.

12. Pop-Up Butterfly – Cinquain

Duplicate butterfly and cinquain sheet for each student. Have students create a cinquain poem about a butterfly. A cinquain is a five line verse with two syllables in its first and last lines, and four, six, and eight syllables in the intervening three lines. Have children color the butterfly and copy their completed poems on the bottom space.

To make the pop-up butterfly folder cut the butterfly wings and head out on the dotted line. Then follow the directions for folding below. Paste the butterfly on construction paper to make a writing folder. The butterfly pops open when the folder is opened.

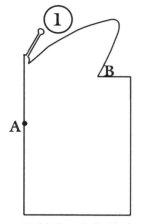

Fold sheet in half after cutting out the butterfly wings and head.

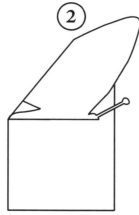

Fold forward from point A to B (shown in first illustration).

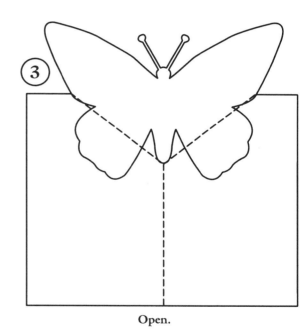

Open.

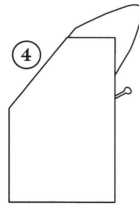

Fold in half again, turning the butterfly to the inside of the fold. Bend paper at both the "V" crease lines and at the center of the butterfly.

Paste the back side of the butterfly sheet to the inside of a construction paper folder. Students may write the title of their poem on the folder cover and then decorate the cover.

They can write their butterfly cinquain on the inside. The butterfly pops open each time the folder is opened.

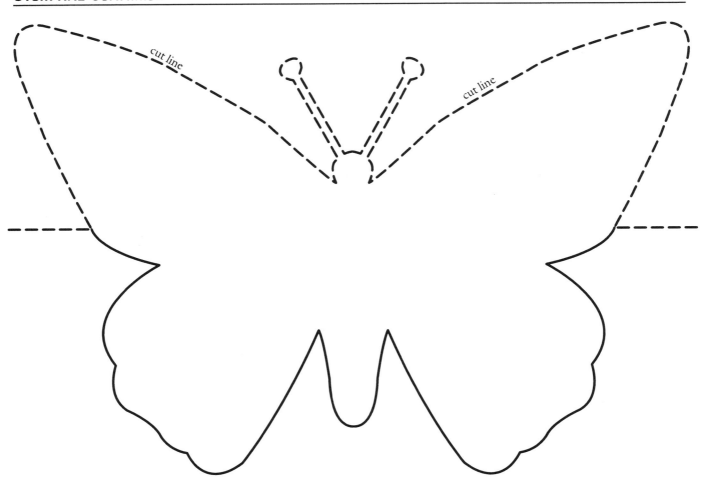

Cinquain

_____
title; 2 syllables; 1 word

_____   _____
4 syllables; 2 words; adjectives

_____   _____
6 syllables; 3 action words (end in "ing")

_____   _____
8 syllables; 4 words that describe feelings

_____   _____
2 syllables; 1 word; synonym of title

Reproduce this page for Butterfly Cinquain. Have students use this page as a guide in writing their butterfly cinquains. When they are happy with their work, have them copy the completed cinquain on the bottom half of the Pop-Up Butterfly on the previous page.

13. Bug Olympics

Follow-up a bug unit with outdoor competitions. Divide your class into teams of five to six students. During each competition the team sends a player. The competition is repeated so each person gets a chance to compete. Some players may have to compete twice if the team is smaller. Each time a player wins a round, the player earns points (3 pts. for lst place; 2 pts. for 2nd place; 1 pt. for 3rd place) for the team. Total the points at the end.

Grasshopper Hop

Mark a starting line and a finish line. Each round has one player from each team. At the "Go!" signal the students hop to the finish line. Award the points as previously described.

Spider Walk

At the "Go!" signal the students walk on all fours from the starting line to the finish line. Direct the students not to crawl on their knees.

Ladybug Toss

Use a jump rope to form a circle in the grass or use chalk on the pavement. Designate a line from which the students will toss the "bug" (bean bag) into the circle or ring. If the bean bag lands in the circle, the player gets three points. If it lands on the line, the player gets two points.

Two-Team Competitions

Ant Egg Relay

Divide the class into two teams. The team members are ants. The teams stand in two lines, one ant in front of the other. The first ants in both teams are given kickballs (ant eggs). If only one ball is available, use a timer to time the competition. At the "Go!" signal, the first ants pass the kickballs backwards over their heads. The second ants receive the balls and pass under their legs to the next in line. The last person rushes to give the ball to the first person. The first to return the ball to the first in line is declared the winner. If a timer is used, stop the watch at the point when the first player receives the ball back. The team with the quickest time wins the game.

Honey Bucket Fill Up

You will need three buckets (two should be the same size), water, and two identical plastic cups. Divide the class into two teams. Tell the students they are honeybees. Place the two buckets of the same size twelve feet from the starting line. Designate which teams receive which buckets. The honey bucket (filled with water) is placed between the two teams. Line up the teams, one student in back of the other, and give the first "bee" from each team a cup. At the "Go!" signal the bees fill their cups with "honey" and rush to the appropriate buckets to empty the cups. They give their cups to the next student in line. At the end measure the water lines. The team with the most "honey" wins. Make sure each team has same the number of bees. A student may have to go twice if the team is small.

14. Mealworm Magic

Purchase some mealworms from a pet store. Place them in a gallon plastic container, half filled with dry bran or oatmeal (food for the mealworms). For moisture place a slice of carrot or potato on top of the cereal. Each day cover the container with a wet paper towel.

The students will be able to observe all stages of metamorphosis except the egg, which is too small to be seen. The mealworm is the larva stage of the beetle. It grows to form the pupa or the cocoon-like stage. The pupa does not eat or move. The adult beetle emerges from this stage to lay eggs and start the life cycle all over again.

Activity 1

Pour the mealworms onto newspaper. Have students find each of the stages: larva, pupa, and adult. Explain that the eggs are too small to see.

Have them count and record on a graph the number of eggs, larva, pupa, and adults. As the students continue the observation and recording every other day, they should begin to see the changes in the numbers on their graphs.

Activity 2

Let your students work in pairs to observe a mealworm with a magnifying glass. They should try to answer the following:

What color is the mealworm?   How long is the mealworm?
How does the mealworm move?   Does it have legs? If yes, how many?
Does it have antennae?   Does it have eyes?
Can you tell your mealworm apart from another team's mealworm?

Activity 3

Use a Venn diagram to discuss the similarities and differences between a larva and a pupa.

Activity 4

Have students illustrate the life cycle of a mealworm on a paper plate.

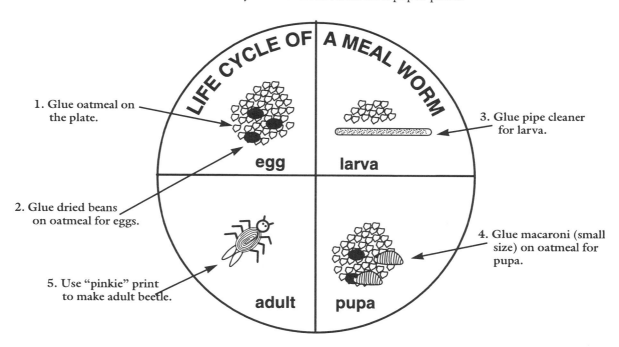

LIFE CYCLE OF A MEAL WORM

1. Glue oatmeal on the plate.

2. Glue dried beans on oatmeal for eggs.

3. Glue pipe cleaner for larva.

4. Glue macaroni (small size) on oatmeal for pupa.

5. Use "pinkie" print to make adult beetle.

egg   larva   adult   pupa

15. Mystery Box

Use a mystery box to provide students with tactile experiences. Make it out of a medium-size cardboard box. Cut a large hole on one side to allow children to touch the items inside the box an arm. Tape a flap over the opening so the students cannot see through the box. Keep the top closed.

Put objects inside for students to feel and determine what they are. Tell them to pretend their hands are antennae. Examples of items you can put in the box: fruit, coin, marshmallow, pencil, eraser, keys, roll of mending tape.

16. Very Hungry Caterpillar – Class Book

Mount the caterpillar below on tagboard, cut out, and laminate. Tape a 12" piece of yarn to the caterpillar. Tape the other end to a 8 ½" X 11" tagboard sheet. This will be the front cover of your class book on the hungry caterpillar. You will need another sheet for the back cover.

Have each student draw a large fruit or vegetable on a 8 ½" X 11" sheet, one page per child. Collect all the papers and laminate. Cut a 2" slit in the center of each drawing. Make it wide enough for the worm to pass through. You can cut the slit by gently folding the paper and cutting.

Bind the book with the caterpillar on the inside of the front cover. Have one of the students add a title and illustrate the cover. Students can weave the caterpillar through the slits.

17. Bee Story

Follow-up *The Bee Tree* with a writing activity. Use the illustration of a bee hive on the next page as a cover for a class book containing creative writing about bees. Have a "brainstorming" session with the entire class and draw a story web on the board to record their ideas.

After the students have decided on the plot and the characters, have them dictate as you write the story on the board. Delegate someone to be responsible for copying the story (several students) and illustrating the pages. This is a good activity to have students do on a computer. Introduce them to the different word processing features that will help them to write a story, including the use of the spell check. Bind the book.

You can also use this cover to bind poems that students have written about bees. See the direction on cinquain (Pop-up Butterfly – Cinquain, pp. 49–51).

18. Chalkboard Quiz

Follow the directions for Lap Chalkboard Quiz (Activity 5, p.33). Have the students prepare for the quiz by visiting the school library media center to locate books about insects, including use of a CD-ROM multimedia encyclopedia. The sample questions pertain to insects:

1. True or false? Insects have four body parts. *(false)*

2. An insect's legs are attached to its .... a. head   b. thorax   c. abdomen *(b)*

3. An insect uses its antennae to .... a. hear and feel   b. hop   c. chew *(a)*

4. Monarch butterflies are poisonous to birds because they eat ....
   a. rose petals   b. nectar   c. milkweed leaves   *(c)*

5. An insect's antennae are attached to its .... a. head b. thorax c. abdomen *(a)*

6. All insects change. This is called .... a. growth b. metamorphosis c. adulthood *(b)*

7. True or false? The stages of metamorphosis are egg, pupa, beetle, larva. *(false)*

8. True or false? The female praying mantis will eat the male praying mantis. *(true)*

9. The female praying mantis lays her eggs in a ....
   a. egg sac   b. web   c. bird nest   *(a)*

10. Praying mantis eat .... a. leaves   b. flowers   c. other insects   *(c)*

11. What does a cricket rub together to make its noise?
    a. Its antennae.   b. Its wings.   c. Its legs.   *(b)*

12. In an ant colony, who lays the eggs?
    a. the queen   b. the workers   c. the king   *(a)*

13. In an ant colony, who does all the work?
    a. the queen   b. the female workers   c. the males   *(b)*

14. What would happen if you put ants from two different colonies in
    the same ant   farm?
    a. They would work together. b. They would be friends.   c. They would fight. *(c)*

15. How many queens does each ant colony have? a. 1   b. 3   c. 5   *(a)*

16. Ants get a sweet liquid by milking a bug called ....
    a. ladybug   b. beetle   c. aphid   *(c)*

17. One insect that can be harmful to people is ....
    a. butterfly b. wasp   c. moth *(b)*

18. Grasshoppers have long back legs to help them ....
    a. hop b. smell c. feel *(a)*

19. True or false? Birds eat insects. *(true)*

20. Butterflies eat ....   a. other insects   b. nectar from flowers   c. leaves   *(b)*

19. Spider Book

Duplicate the pattern below for each student. Cut two circles (same size as the pattern) out of tagboard for each booklet. Have students color, cut out, and paste the picture on a tagboard circle. This will be the front cover of the spider book.

Have students make eight legs out of eight strips of paper folded accordion style (back and front) and have them glue the legs on the back of the second tagboard to form the backs of the books.

Have students write a simple story about a spider or brief information about spiders on pages cut to match the cover. Staple the covers and the pages together.

For legs, fold a strip of paper back and forth, back and forth to make bouncy spider-like legs.

5 Big Red Barn

Big Red Barn

Big Red Barn by Margaret Wise Brown. Harper & Row, 1989. Guess who lives in the big red barn and what are they doing?

Duplicate and cut out the picture of the barn for each student. Fold tagboard or construction paper to make a booklet. Paste the barn at the fold line. The barn may be the cover of the booklet. Cut the tagboard or construction paper in the shape of the barn. Discuss what's inside a board and have the students illustrate the inside of the booklet to look like the inside of a barn. Have the children also locate other books in the library media center about barns. Ask them if they can find pictures of different types of barns.

Paste this edge at the fold

6 Farm Animals

Books to Use

The Cow Who Wouldn't Come Down by Paul Brett Johnson. Orchard Books, 1993. Miss Rosemary's cow ignores her pleas to come back down on the ground as he cavorts in the sky.

The Day Jimmy's Boa Ate the Wash by Trinka Noble. Dial Press,1980. Chaos results when Jimmy takes his pet snake on a field trip to a farm.

Mr. Gumpy's Outing by John Burningham. Henry Holt, 1971. The animals and children on an outing with Mr. Gumpy fall into the water when the boat tips over.

Mule Eggs by Cynthia DeFelice. Orchard Books, 1994. A "city slicker" gets revenge for being tricked by farmer neighbors.

Pig Pig Grows Up by David McPhail. Dutton, 1980. Pig Pig changes his mind about wanting to remain a baby when he receives praise for bravery.

Who Took the Farmer's Hat? by Joan L. Nodset. Harper-Collins, 1963. What happens to the farmer's hat when the wind blows it away? Various animals are not very helpful to the farmer.

Similarities

Cut the sample pictures on the next page out and mount on construction paper. Laminate. Glue magnetic strips to the backs of the pictures.

Place all pictures on a magnetic board. Separate one picture and use it as a starting point. Tell the students that you would like them to select a picture of another animal on the board that has something in common with the starter picture. Have one student start the process of selecting a picture, placing it beside the starter picture, and telling about a similarity between the two. The next student does not have to correlate to the first picture. After all pictures are placed (domino style) on the board, scatter the pictures and select another starter picture.

Sample Student Responses

Both animals have hooves.

Both animals have tails.

Both animals give milk.

Both animals have four feet.

Both animals have feathers.

Both animals lay eggs.

Both animals have beaks.

Both animals have fur.

7 Time for Turkey

Books to Use

One Tough Turkey: A Thanksgiving Story by Steven Kroll. Holiday House, 1982. The Pilgrims, outwitted by Solomon, ate squash instead of turkey.

A Turkey for Thanksgiving by Eve Bunting. Clarion Books, 1991. Turkey is pleasantly surprised when Mr. Moose takes him home for dinner.

Turkey Quiz

Make two copies of the turkey. Hang both turkeys on the chalkboard with magnets. Write Team One and Team Two under the turkeys. Divide the class into two teams. Alternate asking questions to team members using questions related to turkeys. Whenever a student responds correctly, draw a tail feather on the team's turkey. The side with the most tail feathers is declared the winner.

Quiz Questions

1. Do turkeys have teeth? Answer yes or no.   *(no)*

2. Is a turkey a mammal, reptile, or a bird?   *(bird)*

3. Do turkeys have larger eggs than chickens?   *(yes)*

4. Spell turkey.

5. Which is correct? Two turkies or two turkeys.   *(turkeys)*

6. A group of turkeys is called a
   a. herd   b. flock   c. litter   *(b)*

7. Which is the tom turkey, the male or the female?   *(male)*

8. What part of the turkey's body has the wattle?   *(throat)*

9. What part of the turkey's body has spurs?   *(feet)*

10. Which continent has turkeys-Antarctica or North America?   *(North America)*

11. Turkeys eat only plants. Yes or no.   *(no)*

12. Is a turkey a fowl?   *(yes)*

13. Name another animal that is a fowl?

14. Is *One Tough Turkey* a fiction or a nonfiction book?   *(fiction)*

15. A book that gives information about turkeys is a fiction or nonfiction book? *(nonfiction)*

16. Turkeys can only be found on a turkey farm. Yes or no? *(no)*

17. Show a book about turkeys. Have a student identify the title page and point to the author and title.

18. How many feet does a turkey have? *(two)*

19. Does a turkey have a tail? *(yes)*

20. Can you find out about turkeys in an atlas? *(no)*

Turkey Quiz Turkey

cut line

Make two turkeys

Add feathers

8 Egg Roll

Books to Use

Bentley & Egg by William Joyce. HarperCollins, 1992. Kack Kack entrusts her egg to Bentley who must retrieve it from a boy.

The Best Nest by P. E. Eastman. Random House, 1968. Mr. and Mrs. Bird seek out a better home.

Chickens Aren't the Only Ones by Ruth Heller. Grosset & Dunlap, 1981. Beautiful pictures abound of chickens and other animals who lay eggs.

The Egg Tree by Katherine Milhous. Simon & Schuster, 1978. A Caldecott award-winner about a Grandmom's painted eggs, found in an attic, and the start of a tradition for her family.

Goose by Molly Bang. Blue Sky Press, 1996. A baby goose, separated from his mother, finds new friends and learns to fly.

Green Eggs and Ham by Dr. Seuss. Beginner Books, 1960. Sam-I-Am persists in suggesting that everyone should try green eggs and ham.

Horton Hatches the Egg by Dr. Seuss. Random House, 1968. Horton faithfully sits on a lazy bird's egg.

Mule Eggs by Cynthia DeFelice. Orchard Books, 1994. A "city slicker" gets revenge after being tricked by farmer neighbors.

Rechenka's Eggs by Patricia Polacco. Philomel Books, 1988. An injured goose replaces the eggs she breaks and Babushka's kindness with twelve beautifully decorated eggs.

The Talking Eggs: A Folktale from the American South. Retold by Robert D. San Souci. Dial Books, 1989. In this story about two daughters of a widow, the kindness, and the reward the kindness brings, of one sister is contrasted with the selfishness, and subsequent punishment, of her sister.

The Ugly Duckling. Retold by Troy Howell. Putnam, 1990. Retelling of Hans Christian Andersen's tale of an ugly duckling who matures into a beautiful swan.

Other Media

Green Eggs and Ham and Other Stories. 30 min. Columbia Broadcasting Co., 1973. (videocassette)

Chickens Aren't the Only Ones. 30 min. GPN (videocassette) LeVar Burton takes viewers to a hatchery and to Florida to see loggerhead turtles.

Rechenka's Eggs. 30 min. GPN, 1991. (videocassette) Focuses on eggs as an art and scenes of animal babies leaving their eggs.

1. Egg-Rolling Contest

Use plastic eggs for this activity. Divide the class into four teams. There are three competitions, keep the same teams for all three. Give each team six plastic eggs. Mark a starting line with masking tape. Each team will get six tries so if there are only five players, one player must take two turns.

Competition 1

All members of one team roll their eggs from the starting line, one player at a time. Mark the egg that goes the farthest with masking tape. Put the team number on the tape. Give the other eggs back to that team. Continue with the next team. After everyone has had a chance, the team who rolled their egg the farthest, gets five points.

Competition 2

Designate a gate using two pieces of masking tape (12" long) or two rulers. Place the markers parallel to each other and 8" apart on the floor about four feet away from the starting line. Test to see if students can succeed in rolling eggs through the parallel lines. Make adjustments in distance so that the game does not frustrate students but still challenges them.

Students try to roll the eggs through the gate. The egg must pass through the entire 12" to qualify for one point. One point is given to each egg that makes it through the gate.

Competition 3

Collect all eggs except for one from each team. Mark the team number with masking tape on that single egg. Loosen ten other plastic eggs so they can easily come apart. Position them as shown below.

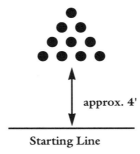

approx. 4'

Starting Line

Have team members roll their team egg and try to break the eggs you have set up. Have teams use the same marked egg each time they roll. For each broken egg (egg that has come apart), the team gets a point. Only reset the eggs in the position shown after each team member from a team has had a turn. Use the same starting point.

Add up the scores: five points for the first place in the first competition, one point each for each egg that rolls through the gate, and one point each for each broken egg.

You may mention that the custom of egg-rolling can be found in some European countries. The egg represents a new life so that egg-rolling is done in the spring (around Easter) when the grass is greener, the leaves start to come out, and the flowers bloom.

2. Egg Trivia

To Make: Cut about twenty eggs out of tagboard. Number the eggs from 1 – 20. Put the numbers 5, 10, 15, 20, and 25 (one number per egg) on the reverse side. Use more 5s, 10s, and 15s than 20s and 25s.

Place eggs on a pocket chart with the numbers 1 – 20 showing in numerical order.

To Play: Divide the class into two teams. Alternate asking questions related to eggs. Each team member who responds correctly gets to pick an egg and earn the points indicated on the back of the egg. Once that egg has been picked and the points recorded, remove it from the pocket chart.

Add the points when all questions have been answered.

Sample Questions

1. Who lays the largest egg?   a. whale   b. ostrich   c. bald eagle   *(b)*
2. Who lays the smallest egg?   a. snake   b. turtle   c. hummingbird   *(c)*
3. Who doesn't lay eggs?   a. duck   b. whale   c. frog   *(b)*
4. Who does lay eggs?   a. alligator   b. giraffe   c. panda   *(a)*
5. Whose eggs are extinct?   *(dinosaur)*
6. Whose eggs are wrapped in a sac?   *(spider)*
7. When the eggs of frogs, toads, and salamanders hatch, what are they called? *(tadpoles)*
8. Yes or no? Eggs have no food value. *(No. Eggs are a source of protein, iron, vitamin A, B, and D.)*
9. Spell the word yolk.
10. What dish's main ingredient is eggs?
    a. omelet   b. taco   c. hot dog   *(a)*
11. How many eggs are in a dozen?   *(12)*
12. Show the book ***Chickens Aren't the Only Ones.***
    Is this a fiction or nonfiction book?   *(nonfiction)*
13. Ask a student to find the title page.
14. Ask another student to point to the title.
15. Ask another student to point to the author's name.
16. Show ***Green Eggs and Ham***. Is this a fiction or nonfiction book?   *(fiction)*
17. Ask student to point to the spine and to the call number. (Using *Green Eggs and Ham*)
18. What does the call number mean? (Using *Green Eggs and Ham*)
    (E is for easy fiction; letters for author)
19. Why do hens sit on their eggs?   *(to keep eggs warm so they hatch)*
20. Spell "nest."
21-23. Ask same questions as in 13–15.

3. Favorite Egg

Have students make a graph of their favorite egg dishes. You might want students to make a quiche or an omelet in your classroom if they are not familiar with those dishes. See the example of an egg graph on the next page.

4. Eggsperiment

Add ½ cup salt to one quart of water. Ask the students what will happen to an egg that is dropped into the water (i.e., float, sink, crack). Make a graph of your students' predictions. Drop the egg into the water. Compare their predictions to the results of this experiment.

5. Eggs in a Basket

Write the numbers 1 – 5 on cardboard eggs, one number per egg. Make about fifteen eggs. Put the eggs in a basket. Have one student at a time pick two eggs from the basket and add the numbers. If the answer is correct, give that person a slip of paper on which to write her/his name. The eggs are returned to the basket.

At the end of this activity draw one slip for a *Lucky Draw* prize.

Examples:

No homework for one night.

Chew gum during _____.

Treat.

Extra _____ minutes on the computer.

Classroom helper during _____.

Lunch with teacher.

6. Green Eggs & Ham

Have the class make an omelet using green vegetables. Use an electric skillet to do this activity.

Have the students decide what green items they would like to have cooked with the eggs. Examples: green pepper, green onions, celery, peas, broccoli, green olives. Serve with ham.

7. Mule Eggs for Sale

Follow-up reading *Mule Eggs* by having students make advertisements to sell mule eggs. Have them visit the school library media center's periodical section and locate different kinds of ads in the magazines. Show examples of ads from fliers that come in the mail. Encourage the students to be creative.

Favorite Eggs Chart

How do you like your eggs cooked?													
scrambled													
hard-boiled													
poached													
omelet													
no way!													
quiche													
sunny side up													
	1	2	3	4	5	6	7	8	9	10	11	12	13

8. Story Starter

Duplicate and enlarge the egg patterns on the next page for each student. You may want to put each egg on a separate sheet. Have students write the sentence:

My egg will hatch into a ...

Direct them to draw a picture of what the egg will hatch into on the blank egg and have them write the word. Have them cut the first egg at the "crack" line. Attach the two cut pieces and the other egg with a brad.

9. Egg Decorating

Duplicate the pattern of an egg on the next page. Direct the students to decorate the egg using the following:

a) a zigzag line

b) a straight line

c) parallel lines

d) a curvy line

e) circles

f) triangles

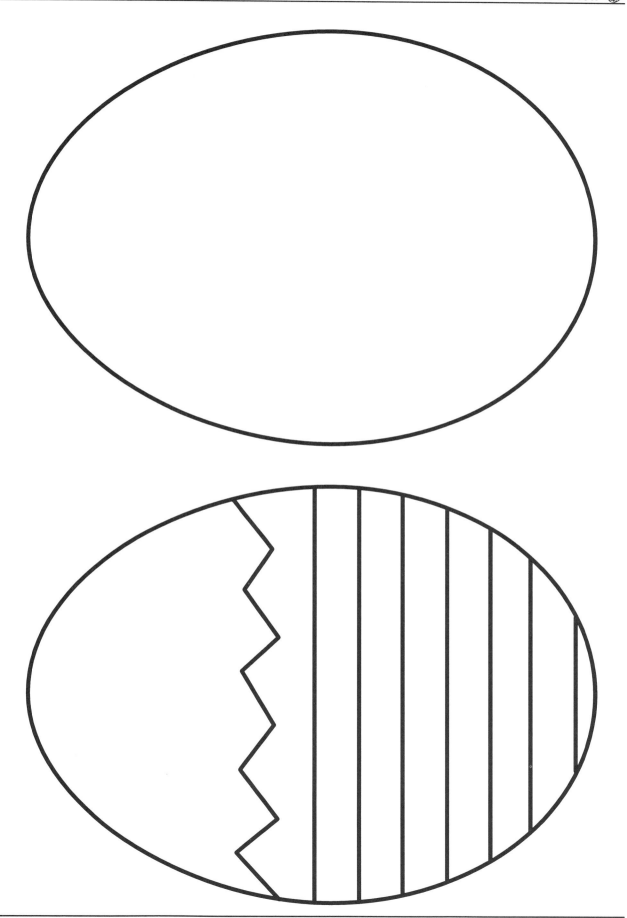

9 Something to Do About the Weather

Books to Use

The Black Snowman by Phil Mendez. Scholastic Inc., 1989. A magic kente empowers a snowman to help Jacob save his brother.

Bringing the Rain to Kapiti Plain: A Nandi Tale. Retold by Verna Aardema. Dial, 1981. Ki-Pat uses his bow and arrow to help bring back the rain in Kapiti Plain.

Cloudy With a Chance of Meatballs by Judy Barrett. Atheneum, 1978. The people of Chewandswallow are faced with the problem of left-over food that falls from the sky.

Dandelion by Don Freeman. Puffin, 1964. A lion's friends do not recognize him when he comes to a party with a new hairdo and dressed in dapper clothes.

Hurricane by David Wiesner. Clarion, 1990. A tree, downed by a hurricane, becomes a jungle, a ship, and a space ship for two brothers.

It Looked Like Spilt Milk by Charles G. Shaw. HarperCollins, 1947. Sometimes clouds look like birds, a rabbit, a flower, and spilt milk.

Mirandy and Brother Wind by Patricia McKissack. Knopf, 1988. Brother Wind helps a girl and a clumsy boy win the cakewalk dance competition.

The Mitten. Retold by Jan Brett. Putnam, 1989; and *The Mitten.* Retold by Alvin Tresselt. Lothrop, Lee & Shepard, 1964. Various animals squeeze into a mitten to escape the cold.

Mushroom in the Rain by Mirra Ginsburg. Macmillan, 1987. A mushroom keeps expanding to provide shelter for animals escaping the rain.

The Snowy Day by Ezra Jack Keats. Puffin, 1976. Although Peter ends one wonderful day in the snow with a melted snowball, he wakes up to another snowy day.

Thomas' Snowsuit by Robert Munsch. Annick Press, 1985. Thomas's persistence in not wearing his snowsuit frustrates his teacher and principal.

Umbrella by Taro Yashima. Viking, 1985. In this story a young Japanese girl listens to the sound of raindrops on her umbrella.

White Snow, Bright Snow by Alvin Tresselt. Lothrop, Lee & Shepard, 1947. Caldecott award-winner about the effects of snow on people and animals.

The Wind Blew by Pat Hutchins. Macmillan, 1974. An umbrella, balloon, shirt, kite, and letters are among the things the wind blows away.

Other Media

Bringing the Rain to Kapiti Plain. 30 min. GPN, 1988. (videocassette) LeVar Burton focuses on meteorology as a science and occupation.

Hurricane: Storm Science. "Inside a Hurricane" (website) <http://www.miamisci.org/hurricane/hurricane0.html> See Hurricane Survival Kit list in this site (hurrican/list.html).

The Snowman. 26 Min. Sony, 1982. (videocassette) A boy is taken to the North Pole by his snowman.

The Snowy Day: Stories and Poems. 30 min. GPN. (videocassette) *Reading Rainbow* feature on winter fun and winter sports.

Windows on Science. Vol. II. Optical Data Corporation, 1990. (laser disk) Section on weather includes information on hurricanes, tornadoes, and other storms.

1. What's the Weather?

Write the words below on the board as shown:

SUNNY DAY   SNOWY DAY   RAINY DAY   WINDY DAY

Listed are some words a forecaster may use in his or her weather forecast. Have the students locate the meaning of the words in the library's dictionary. Read these words aloud to the class and have the students decide on which days those words would most likely be used. Write the words under the headings as students direct you. Do not use those words that may be too difficult for your class. Some words may be put under more than one heading.

Sample Words

fair	blizzard	downpour	blustery
cloudburst	sleet	hail	slick roads
scorcher	clear	icy	flurries
breezy	drizzle	wind chill	sunshine
showers	gusty	balmy	sprinkle

2. It Looks Like ... ?

Read the book *It Looked Like Spilt Milk.* Give each student white construction paper and direct the students to draw large, simple shapes of their own choice. Have them slowly tear along the lines they've drawn to create rough-edged shapes like the one shown here.

whale

torn shape

When they have completed their "clouds," paste them on blue construction paper, one shape per page. Have them write

> *Sometimes it looked like a _____.   But it wasn't a _____.*

Bind the pages into a class book. As an alternative you can have them paste cotton balls on their shapes, and put the pages up on a bulletin board.

3. Don't Melt the Snowmen!

Draw two snowmen on the board. Put team numbers under the snowmen. Next to each snowman put the temperature levels as shown. Pick a student to be the sun and divide the class into teams.

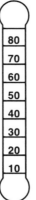

Team 1

Team 2

Write the words from the lists below on the board large enough for the class to see. Have the team members (pick one student from each team) decide which is correct.

If the response is correct, nothing is done to the snowman. If incorrect, the sun "melts" the lowest part of the snowman with an eraser.

The winning snowman is the one that is most intact at the end of the game.

Questions

Which is the correct spelling?
1. two snowmans or two snowmen
2. three snowballs or three snowballes
3. two scarfs or two scarves?
4. four buttons or four buttones
5. icy or icee
6. sled or slead
7. mittens or mittenes
8. boots or bootes
9. earmuffs or earsmuff
10. skis or skies
11. coats or coates
12. snowee or snowy
13. sockes or socks

What is the missing letter?
14. Jan__ary
15. wint__r
16. holida__
17. snowsu __t
18. Februar__
19. shov __l
20. gl__ve

4. Weather Report

Follow-up reading *Hurricane* by having students write a weather report about an imaginary hurricane. Videotape their reports to have them see each other as weather reporters. They may do a telecast about an impending hurricane, about safety information, or about the after-effects of a disastrous hurricane.

5. Signs of the Seasons – Group Project

Divide the class into four to five groups. Give each group a large posterboard and several magazines. Direct the students to label their posterboards with the four seasons. Have the students delegate responsibilities for the project—hunting pictures, illustrating, cutting, pasting, labeling, and reporting. Have them cut or draw pictures of clothing, recreational objects (such as football, baseball, skis), or things from nature (leaves, flowers) to paste under the proper labels. The purpose of this activity is for the group members to work cooperatively and to be creative in this assignment.

The reporter from each group presents his or her group's project to the entire class. In a separate report to the teacher the reporter should indicate who was responsible for each task and whether that student completed his or her task (self-evaluation).

Spring	Summer
Winter	Fall

6. Sounds of the Weather – Group Project

Follow-up reading *Umbrella* by Taro Yashima (Viking, 1985) with this activity. In the story a Japanese girl listens to the sounds of raindrops on her umbrella.

Divide the class into four to five groups and give them the task of coming up with the best way to emulate the sounds of raindrops, thunder, wind, hail, sleet, or snow. The students may hum, whistle, use musical instruments, or act in their presentation to the entire group.

7. Sequence Activity

Cut out the pictures on the next page to use with *The Wind Blew*. Mount on tagboard or construction paper. Place the pictures on a sentence or pocket chart. Read the book. While you are reading, have students tell you what the wind will blow away next. There are clues in the illustrations. Have students direct you on how to get the pictures in story order.

Cut out the *Wind Blew* pictures and have students put the m in the sequence of the events in the story.

8. Dictionary Fun

Duplicate the Dictionary Quiz – Weather sheet (p. 76) for each student. Divide the class into groups of four. Group members will search for dictionary definitions. Groups should meet first to decide who in their group will look-up each of the weather terms. Each person must look up at least one word. Groups are responsible for researching all words. They may help those students who have difficulty in locating a word. Groups should also select a recorder for during the competition part of the activity.

Give the class fifteen minutes to look up the words and to discuss the definitions with each other. Give each group a lap chalkboard, chalk, and an eraser.

When the research time is up, have the class compete by completing the sentences in the Dictionary Fun Quiz below. Have the recorders write the word (from the list) that best fits into the sentence. After each sentence is read, give the command "Boards up!" The recorder holds up the board to show the group's answer. Each group with the correct answer gets a point. Give the second direction "Boards down, erase!" Continue with the next sentence. Count the points.

Dictionary Fun Quiz Sentences (Have recorder write just the weather word when sentence is read.)

1. When the wind begins to _____, let's fly our kites. *(bluster)*
2. The _____ shows that a storm is on the way. *(barometer)*
3. The _____ made the road icy. *(sleet)*
4. The mildew was caused by _____ weather. *(humid)*
5. James studies _____ to learn to forecast weather. (meteorology)
6. Many were injured in India because of a _____. *(cyclone)*
7. Sometimes you can't see the stars at night because of the _____. *(smog)*
8. I was caught in a _____ and got soaking wet. *(cloudburst)*
9. The _____ will turn to snow if the temperature gets colder. *(sleet)*
10. A _____ helps a meteorologist forecast the weather. *(barometer)*
11. My basement is _____ and the books stored *(humid)* there are full of _____. *(mildew)*
12. A _____ destroyed a little village in Asia. *(cyclone)*
13. The speaker seems to _____ when he talks. *(bluster)*
14. I stayed indoors because the _____ made me cough and hurt my eyes. *(smog)*
15. Now that the _____ is over, we can go out to play. *(cloudburst)*

Dictionary Quiz – Weather

Decide which words each group member look up in the dictionary. Each person must look up at least one word. Help each other if necessary. Select a person to be the group's recorder. Discuss the definitions when all have completed their tasks and every word has been researched.

During the chalkboard competition, work together to decide on the word that best fits the missing word in the sentence.

Locate the definitions of the following words:

1. bluster

2. barometer

3. sleet

4. humid

5. meteorology

6. cyclone

7. smog

8. cloudburst

9. Snowman Treat

Have each student make a snowman by attaching three large-size marshmallows with a toothpick. They may stick toothpicks at the sides for arms. Use marshmallow creme as glue to attach gumdrops and/or raisins for eyes and buttons.

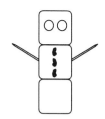

10. Finger-Painting With Shaving Cream

Have students play in the snow with shaving cream. Put a gob of shaving cream on paper for each child to paint with as in finger-painting.

11. Winter Scene

Use the sample winter picture on the next page to have students discuss a day in the snow. You can use this as a follow-up to *A Snowy Day*.

12. Snow Wash

Prepare a wash mixture of one part white tempera to three parts of water. Have students use crayons to draw and color a snow scene on blue construction paper. Use a brush to "white-wash" the picture. The crayon will resist the wash. Put pictures up on the bulletin board.

13. Snowflake

Show your students how to cut a snowflake. Fold the paper in half. Fold in half again. Fold diagonally and cut diagonally as shown:

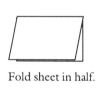

Fold sheet in half.

Fold in half again.

Fold diagonally.

Cut shape along open bottom edge.

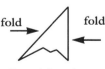

fold   fold

Remaining piece should have two fold edges.

Cut shapes from the fold edges.

Unfold.

14. Dance Show

Follow-up *Mirandy and Brother Wind* by having students demonstrate their dancing talent. Have them dance individually, with a partner, or with a small group. You may need to prepare them in advance so they can have their music ready. Ask for volunteers for this activity as not all students will feel comfortable in performing.

15. Mushroom in the Rain

Follow-up *Mushroom in the Rain* by having students draw and color animals under the mushroom waiting for the rain to end. This would be a good opportunity to use a CD-ROM multimedia encyclopedia in the library to show students how to use this resource to locate pictures on different types of mushrooms.

16. Let's Make Rain (Demonstration)

You will need:
a cookie sheet,
ice cubes,
a small pan,
hot plate,
4 - two liter bottles.

Directions

Fill a pan half full of water. Place the pan on a hot plate and heat to boiling. Make a platform above the pan by placing a two liter bottle at each corner of the hot plate and resting a cookie sheet on top of the bottles. Put ice cubes on the cookie sheet.

Watch what happens. The water begins to boil and turns to water vapor. The water vapor rises into the air over the pan. When the warm air hits the cold cookie sheet, the warm air begins to cool. Cool air can't hold much water vapor. Some of the water vapor from the pan begins to change back into tiny droplets of water. The droplets of water come together on the bottom of the cookie sheet. When the droplets of water get big enough and heavy enough, it will "rain" over the pan.

17. Blinding Blizzard

Have students practice giving directions and following directions. Blindfold one student and have the other students give the blindfolded student directions to places in the room (e.g., sink, chalkboard, door). They should give commands using such words as left, right, forward, backward, and the number of steps to take in the particular direction.

Look Who's Hiding from the Rain

10 Terrible Trolls

Book to Use

Trouble With Trolls by Jan Brett. Putnam, 1992. Treva bargains with some trolls to get her dog back.

Troll Lore

Don't go out at night if you're in Norway. The mountain trolls may be out doing mischief. You don't want to be kidnapped or changed into an animal. You're safe in the daylight. Sunshine makes the trolls turn into stone, so the trolls hide in the mountains when the sun is out.

There are trolls who live in trees, and trolls who live under bridges. Remember the troll who pestered the Three Billy Goats Gruff?

There are trolls with one head, and trolls with three or more heads. A head may be tucked under their arms. The meanest of all are the trolls with twelve heads. They are bad-tempered because the heads are always arguing and snarling at each other. Those trolls have headaches all the time.

The hair on those heads is shaggy, never brushed or washed. Bushes, weeds, and even trees sprout from their heads, noses, and ears. It's not uncommon for a bird to build a nest in that mess. Imagine having a nose so long, a troll-hag (woman) uses it to stir while cooking.

Trolls have cow tails and fur all over their bodies. The rumbling sounds you might hear may not be thunder. The trolls may be dancing or wrestling with each other.

They spend many quiet moments sitting on a stack of gold and silver. Trolls have plenty, thanks to the gnomes who mine in the mountains. They love their silver and gold and never spend it. That's why they are so rich. Their second love is playing tricks on the poor people who meet up with these terrible mischief makers.

Looking at Illustrations

As you read and show the pages of this book, *Trouble With Trolls,* have students look for the following items: (Put the list of the items on the board before reading)

1. cross stitch
2. hedgehog
3. slingshot
4. bellows
5. pom-pom
6. stool
7. bells
8. heart designs
9. chimney
10. beetle

Discuss trolls, and compare the clothing of Treva with the clothes worn by the trolls. Discuss the types of containers used by the trolls in their home.

11 Programs for Plants

Books to Use

Blueberries for Sal by Robert McCloskey. Puffin, 1976. A mix-up occurs when Sal and her mother, and a mother bear and her cub pick blueberries.

Carrot Seed by Ruth Krauss. HarperCollins, 1945. A carrot seed planted by a little boy grows even though no one in his family believed it would.

A Friend for Dragon by Dav Pilkey. Orchard, 1991. A dragon is frustrated in his attempts to befriend an apple.

The Giving Tree by Shel Silverstein. HarperCollins, 1964. A tree denies nothing to a boy it dearly loves.

The Legend of the Bluebonnet: An Old Tale of Texas. Retold by Tomie de Paola. Putnam, 1983. She-Who-Is-Alone gives her only possession, a doll, to end a drought.

Legend of the Indian Paintbrush. Retold by Tomie de Paola. New York:Putnam, 1988. Paint brushes, left on a hill by an artist, become the Indian paintbrush flower.

The Lotus Seed by Sherry Garland. Harcourt Brace, 1993. The lotus seed, plucked by a grandmother for a special purpose, becomes a part of her family in a new country.

Miss Rumphius by Barbara Cooney. Viking, 1982. Following her grandfather's advise, Miss Rumphius tries to do something to make the world beautiful.

Mushroom in the Rain by Mirra Ginsburg. Macmillan, 1987. More animals seek shelter from the rain under a mushroom that must keep expanding.

Poppy Seeds by Clyde R. Bulla. Puffin, 1994. A Mexican boy envisions a village of beautiful flowers when he receives a gift of flower seeds.

Too Many Pumpkins by Linda White. Holiday House, 1996. A woman's dislike of pumpkins changes when she has great fun entertaining her neighbors with them.

Tops & Bottoms. Adapted by Janet Stevens. Harcourt Bracey, 1995. By outwitting Lazy Bear, Hare manages to feed his hungry family.

Other Media

Fun With Fruits and Vegetables Kids Cookbook (website)
<http:www.dole5aday.com/cook/4.html>

Magic School Bus Goes to Seed. 30 min. KidVision, 1995. (video) Plants are featured in this Magic School Bus adventure.

1. Traveling With Miss Rumphius

Follow-up reading *Miss Rumphius* by having students work with the atlas and encyclopedia. You will need to be divide the class into smaller groups and have several atlases on hand. They will also need to use an encyclopedia.

Assign each group the task of locating places where Miss Rumphius might have been. At the end of a designated time have each group report on their research. Each group needs to have a recorder and a reporter.

Find: (Recorders write the information.)

1. A city by the sea _____

2. A tropical island _____

3. A tall mountain where the snow never melts (over 15,000 ft.) _____

4. Jungle area (or a tropical rain forest) _____

5. Desert _____

6. A place where lions live (Look in the encyclopedia) _____

7. A place where kangaroos hop (encyclopedia) _____

8. A place where camels live (encyclopedia) _____

Have the reporter report on the group's answers. There should be a variety of answers for most of the places.

2. Make the World Beautiful

After reading *Miss Rumphius,* have the students discuss what they would do to make the world beautiful. Ask them to name the most beautiful thing they ever saw. Give each child a sheet of paper with a line across it to represent a hill or the horizon. Have them decorate the page with flowers, trees, and animals to make the scenery beautiful.

3. The Carrot Seed

Follow-up *The Carrot Seed* by having students change the characters and the vegetable that finally grows. They may also be creative in their response to the little boy (or girl). For example, they may say, "Good luck, kid!" instead of "It won't come up."

4. Scatter BINGO – Plants

Duplicate the blank BINGO sheet and the picture squares for each student. Have students cut out the picture squares. Play BINGO by having students place nine pictures on their boards. They must not move any picture until someone has called BINGO. They may change the pictures and the arrangement on the board before the next round begins.

Use dried beans for markers. If some of the illustrations are confusing to the students, discuss each of the vegetables are before starting the game.

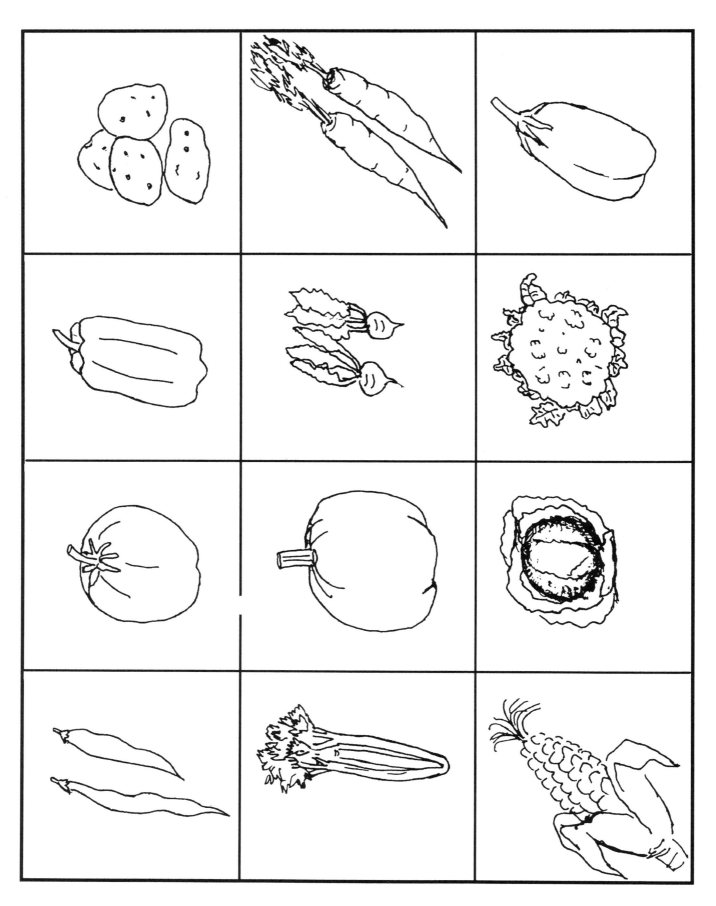

PLANTS **BINGO**

5. Pumpkin Pie

Read a story that relates to pumpkins. Have students look in *Guiness' Book of World Records* to find the size of the largest pumpkin on record. Then have the students make a pumpkin pie using the following recipe for three "no bake" pumpkin pies. Get the necessary ingredients and utensils for the class. Put the recipe on the board.

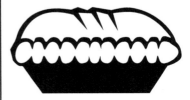

> *Recipe for No Bake Pumpkin Pie*
>
> *1 cup canned pumpkin*
> *1 package instant vanilla pudding*
> *1 cup Cool Whip*
> *2/3 cup milk*
> *3/4 teaspoon pumpkin pie spice*
> *1 teaspoon cinnamon*
> *1 Graham cracker crust pie shell*
>
> *Mix all ingredients. Pour into the pie shell. Freeze for several hours.*

Divide the class into three groups. Have each group follow the directions, one group at a time, to make a pie. The smaller groups will allow more hands-on experiences for each student and the teacher will not need to have duplicates of needed cooking utensils. Within each group, students need to decide who will be responsible for measuring, stirring, cleaning, and serving.

Mark the bottoms of the pie pans with the groups' numbers. Put the pies in the freezer for several hours. Have the groups decide what staff members (e.g., principal, custodian, secretary, itinerant teacher, media specialist) will be given the extra pie slices. See if students can tell you the directions for making the pie.

6. Blueberry Treat

Follow-up *Blueberries for Sal* by having a blueberry snack for the students. Examples: crackers with blueberry jelly, blueberry Pop-tart, blueberry muffin.

7. What Is It?

Have students taste an unusual fruit or vegetable and have them describe it and its taste. Have them discuss whether it is a fruit or vegetable. Examples: lichee, mango, papaya, beans sprouts, artichokes.

8. Chalkboard Quiz – Plants

Divide the class into five groups. In preparation for the following quiz, have them research plants to find basic facts about plants. Students may use a variety of information sources (encyclopedias, websites, dictionaries, etc.) to locate information. Give each group a lap chalkboard (chalkboard slate), a chalk, and an eraser. Designate the team recorder. Read a question. The recorder writes the team answer reached by the consensus of the group. The answer will either be true or false, or a letter. At the "Boards Up!" command, the recorder shows the answer. Each team with the correct answer gets a point. The recorder follows the "Boards Down, Erase!" command and waits for the next question.

Sample Plant Questions

1. What do all plants need?
    a. sunlight and water   b. bees to pollinate   c. insecticides   *(a)*

2. True or false? The leaf is the main food-making part of the plant. *(true)*

3. True or false? Leaves are important as food for animals and plants. *(true)*

4. True or false? Leaves help us breathe. *(true)*

5. What gives a leaf its green color?
    a. sun rays   b. pollen   c. chlorophyll *(c)*

6. Where is water absorbed from?   a. the stem b. the bark c. the roots   *(c)*

7. The main part of a leaf is called the   a. stem b. blade c. bark   *(b)*

8. True or false? Plants don't need air since it gives off oxygen. *(false)*

9. The process of making food for the plant is called ....

    a. photosynthesis   b. growth   c. pollination *(a)*

10. True or false? Leaves have different patterns. *(true)*

11. True or false? All leaves turn colors in the autumn.   *(false)*

12. What is the name of a tree whose leaves do not turn colors in the fall?

    a. annual   b. evergreen   c. permagreen   *(b)*

13. True or false? All plants need the same amount of water and sunlight. *(false)*

14. True or false? Stems carry water and minerals from the roots to the leaves. *(true)*

15. True or false? Bees are the only animals that carry pollen from flower to flower. *(false)*

9. What is My Favorite Vegetable?

Survey the students to see what is their favorite vegetable. There is a sample survey sheet on the next page. You can change the sheet to include other vegetables or fruits.

10. Vegetable Soup Game

Select about six vegetables and write their names on small cards, one vegetable per card. You will need a spinner or dice to play this game. Divide the class into two groups. Pick one of the cards. Have a player from one team try to guess the name of the vegetable by asking for a letter. "Is there an 'a' in the word?" the player may ask.

If there is, the player spins the spinner or tosses the dice. The number shown is the point value of that letter. If the letter appears more than once, that team gets double points. Put the letter on the board. If the answer is "no," the team does not get any points. Alternate turns. At any point during a team's turn, that team can try to guess the word. If correct, that team gets an additional ten points. If incorrect, that team automatically loses that round.

Examples of vegetables: eggplant, cucumber, cabbage, potato, broccoli, celery, zucchini, asparagus, onion, lettuce.

What Is Your Favorite Vegetable?

beans

broccoli

carrots

corn

lettuce

peas

potato

11. Book Report

Have students watch the *Reading Rainbow* video *The Lotus Seed* to see examples of oral book reports given by children. Direct the students to locate a plant-related fiction or folktale book in the library, read it, and give an oral book report.

12. Plant Cycle

Cut strips of paper 1" X 5 ½", four strips per student. Explain the plant cycle. Have students write on the strips, one word per strip, the words: seed, sprout, flower, fruit. Have them glue the strips together as a chain in the order shown.

seed	flower
sprout	fruit

13. Simple Plant Experiments

Three Bean Experiment: Place three beans between moist paper towel for each student. Put the towel in a sandwich-size plastic Zip-Lock bag. Write each person's name on their bag. Close the bags and place on a tray near the window. The students will be excited to see their bean plants grow.

Color Dyes Experiment: Get two white carnations. Place one in plain water and one in water colored with red or blue dye. The students will observe the effect of the dye on the flower.

14. Plant Booklet

Make booklets using the pattern on the next page. Have students research and write a few sentences about the parts of a plant on the designated pages.

Cut two 4" X 12" pieces of white construction paper for each student. Fold the ends over as shown below so that the second one fits into the first. Staple the booklet to a colored sheet of construction paper 4¾" X 9". Then staple to the flower pattern on the next page.

Write the words flower, leaves, stem, and root on the bottom of each of the pages. Have students write about each item on the appropriate page.

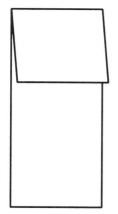

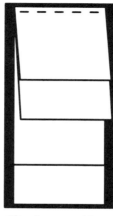

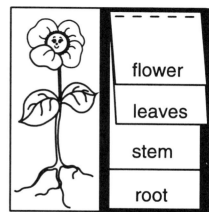

Fold the first
strip over 3¼".

Fold the second
strip over 5".

Slip the second into
the first & staple to
construction paper.

Label pages as shown and have
students write about the items on the
appropriate pages.

Copy flower onto plain paper and
trim top and bottom so that page
is 9" tall. Paste Plant Booklet
pages next to flower so that the
parts of the flower line up with the
appropriate description.

15. GRASS HEADS

Punch one hole in the bottom of each Styrofoam cup required for the students. Fill the cups with dirt. Plant grass seeds and periodically water the seeds. When the grass begins to grow, have the students color, cut, and tape faces around the cups. Have them also cut out ears from construction paper, glue them to the side of the cups, and bend them forward so they will stick out. The grass will serve as the hair.

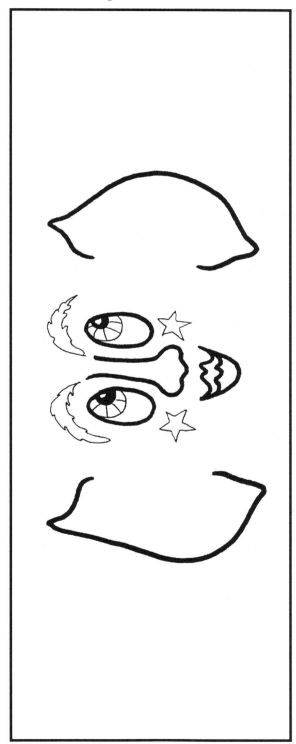

Aesop's Fables – Skits

Aesop's Fables by Arnold Lobel. HarperCollins, 1980.

Aesop's Fables. Retold by Anne Gatti. Gulliver Books, 1992.

Have students do simple skits with Aesop's fables. Explain that a fable is a short story with a moral or lesson at the end. Frequently the characters are animals. Have students search in the library's card or computer catalog to see if they can locate other books on fables.

We have included several Aesop's fables that we have rewritten for you to read to your students. Have them act out the stories using simple props.

Props

The Miller, His son, and Their Donkey: The only prop needed for "The Miller, His Son, and Their Donkey" is a stick horse (pattern on p. 93). You can either purchase a stick horse or make one by attaching a horse's face to a yardstick. A pattern for the head of a stick horse can be found on the next page. Have the miller, his son, and the donkey walk in a circle as they encounter the other characters. Either read the story or have one of your students be the narrator.

The Shepherd Boy and the Wolf: A sample of the prop needed for the wolf in "The Shepherd Boy and the Wolf" is provided on p. 95. Have the wolf character wear it as a band around his/her head. The pasture may be a table on which the shepherd boy sits.

The Grasshopper and the Ant: Have the students make finger puppets (p. 97) for "The Grasshopper and the Ant." Ask for volunteers to retell the story to you using the finger puppets. Encourage your students to find someone to share the story with at home.

The Miller, His Son, and Their Donkey

A poor miller and his son were on their way to the fair to sell their only donkey. The miller walked on one side of the donkey, while his son walked on the other side.

They met two girls returning home from the fair.

"Look at them!" said one of the girls. "How foolish to walk when one of them could be riding."

"Silly people!" the other girl called out. Both girls giggled.

The miller did not want people to think he was foolish so he said, "My son, get up on the donkey, and I will walk." He helped his son get on the donkey.

They had not gone far when they passed two old men. The two men looked at them in disgust. "Young man, you should be the one walking—not your father," scolded one of the old men.

Stick Horse Directions

Enlarge and duplicate pattern. Trace the outline
of the horse's features on the other side of the
sheet. Duplicate each side so that you have two
copies of the horse head. Color, cut and staple
the pattern pieces together to make a two-sided
puppet head. You can stuff the head with paper
to give it more shape. Leave an opening at the
base of the neck to slip in a yardstick or pole.

The second one agreed. "Yes, lazy boy, get down and let your poor father ride!"

The miller's son did not want people to think he was lazy, so he quickly got off the donkey.

"Father, you ride and I'll walk," the son said. His father got on the donkey.

A little farther on they passed a woman and her children. By the frown on her face and her hands on her hips, the miller knew she was angry. "Shame on you!" yelled the woman. "Riding while your poor boy has to walk. How can you do that?"

The miller was embarrassed by her yelling, he got off the donkey.

"This time let's both ride," said the miller. "No one can say anything with both of us riding. Both climbed on the donkey.

He was wrong.

As they passed the bakery, the baker stepped out of his shop to scold them.

"Hey you!" he called out. "Look at your poor donkey barely able to carry the both of you. You two can better carry him that he can carry you —you cruel people!"

They did not want people to think of them as cruel so they quickly got off the donkey.

"We must carry the donkey," the miller said, "then people will not think of us as cruel."

They tied the donkey's legs together and used a pole across their shoulders to carry the donkey to the fair.

As they crossed the bridge that led to the fair people started laughing. They laughed so hard that the miller and his son lost their balance. All three fell into the water.

No one wanted to buy a donkey that had to be carried.

The lesson to this story is that if you try to please everyone, you will please no one.

The Shepherd Boy and the Wolf

Every day a young shepherd boy took his father's sheep to the mountain pasture to graze. He was full of mischief and liked to play. He did not like being alone, far away from anyone, guarding the sheep. He thought of a way to have a little fun.

He ran down to the village and cried, "Help! Help! A wolf! A wolf!"

The villagers stopped their work to grab hoes, pitchforks, and clubs. They rushed with him to the pasture.

"Where's the wolf?" they asked.

The shepherd boy laughed, "It's only a joke!"

The villagers were both glad there was no wolf and angry that they ran for nothing.

That was so much fun for the boy that he decided to try again.

"Help! Help! A wolf! A wolf!" the boy screamed as he ran into the village.

The villagers again ran up to the pasture to help. The shepherd boy laughed even more. "Tricked again!" he teased the villagers. The villagers stomped back home.

Then one day as the shepherd boy lay on his back thinking of another joke to play on the villagers, a vicious wolf appeared. It snarled at the boy and chased the sheep.

The frightened shepherd boy ran down to the village yelling, "Help! Help! A wolf! A wolf!"

Wolf Mask Directions

Cut 1½"-wide strip of tagboard to make
a headband for the wolf mask. Cut out
wolf face and attach ends of the
headband to sides of wolf's face. Adjust
the length of the tagboard strip to fit
child's head.

The villagers said, "He's doing it again. Let's pay no attention to him."

No matter how much the boy pleaded for help, no one stopped their work. The boy returned to the pasture to find his sheep all gone. The wolf ate some of the sheep and the rest ran away.

The shepherd boy learned a lesson.

Liars will not be believed even when they tell the truth.

The Ant and the Grasshopper

"Play, play, play! I'm gonna play all day." That's what the grasshopper said, and that's what the grasshopper did. He didn't work — not one bit!

One day Grasshopper saw an ant tugging and pushing, tugging and pushing.

"What do you have there, Mr. Ant?" he asked.

"Oh, Mr. Grasshopper, I'm so glad you came along. I'm trying to carry this kernel of corn to my cupboard. But it's so big and I'm so small. Do you think you could give me a hand?" questioned the ant.

"Work? on a fine summer day like this? Not me!" and off Grasshopper went singing, "Play, play, play! I'm gonna play all day!" That's what the grasshopper said, and that's what the grasshopper did.

But Ant didn't give up. He knew when winter came food would be hard to find. So he worked and worked until he finally got that kernel of corn into his cupboard.

The next day Grasshopper was at it again — playing, playing, playing. And Ant was at it again — working, working, working.

"Say, Ant, what's that you're dragging along today?" Grasshopper asked.

"Oh, Grasshopper, I found this bread crumb. I'm taking it to my cupboard, too. I'm storing up food for the winter, you know," Ant replied.

"Winter," chuckled the grasshopper. "You don't think about winter when it's summertime! Come on, Little Ant, I'll show you how to have fun."

But the little ant went right on dragging that bread crumb. He wasn't going to let the cold winter catch him without food.

"Grasshopper," the ant scolded, "you'd better start thinking about winter while it's summertime. Otherwise you'll be thinking about food while it's wintertime."

"Oh, phooey!" chirped the grasshopper. And he hopped away singing his favorite tune, "Play, play, play! I'm gonna play all day." That's what the grasshopper said, and that's what the grasshopper did.

But summer didn't last forever. Soon the days became bitter cold. Snow covered the ground. And just as Ant had predicted, it was wintertime and Grasshopper found himself thinking of *food!* There was no food to be found. Grasshopper's tummy was empty and rumbly. He was ever so hungry!

"Oh how I wish I'd listened to that ant," he thought. "Playing is not much fun when you're starving."

Poor, hungry Grasshopper hopped here and there and everywhere searching for food.

In his search he stumbled upon the ant's house. Grasshopper peeked in the window. What do you think he saw? Ant's cupboard door was open. The shelves were stuffed with delicious food—enough to last the whole winter. On the table was ant's plate, piled high with corn and bread. And Ant, with his full tummy bulging, was dancing around his table singing, "Play, play, play! I'm gonna play all day!" That's what the ant said, and that's what the ant did!

There's a time for work, and there's a time for play.

Finger Puppet Directions

1. Duplicate puppets on tagboard for each student.

2. Have students color puppets.

3. Cut along the outside edge of dotted lines.

4. Fold along the center line.

5. Fold tabs A and B over edge C and glue the tabs down.

6. Have students stick their fingers inside the "envelopes" and retell the story.

 **Caps and Hats and Things on Your Head**

Books to Use

Aunt Flossie's Hats (and Crab Cakes Later) by Elizabeth Fitzgerald Howard. Houghton Mifflin, 1991. Memories of Sundays at Aunt Flossie's, trying on her hats that too had memories.

Caps For Sale: A Tale of a Peddler, Some Monkeys, and Their Monkey Business by Esphyr Slobodkina. Scholastic, 1993. Monkeys steal the peddler's caps and mimics his actions.

The Hat by Jan Brett. G. P. Putnam's Sons, 1997. A hedgehog amuses other animals with his explanation of why the stocking is stuck on his head.

Hats, Hats, Hats by Ann Morris. Lothrop, Lee & Shepard, 1989. Photos of hats from different countries. Index in back briefly explains hats.

Who Took the Farmer's Hat? by Joan L. Nodset. HarperCollins, 1963. What happens to the farmer's hat when the wind blows it away? Various animals are not helpful to the farmer.

Whose Hat? by Margaret Miller. Greenwillow Books, 1988. Children are shown wearing various hats (cowhand, pirate, construction worker, etc.)

1. Match Game

Duplicate the match game on the next page. Cut out the pictures and mount them on tagboard squares. Laminate the pictures. Place them on a pocket chart, pictures facing the chart. Have students take turns turning two cards over to get a match. If they do make a match, the student tells who would wear that particular hat. Shuffle the cards and place the cards back on the chart if all students have not had a turn.

2. Skit

Using the pattern on the next page, make enough caps for each child to have. Cut them out of red, brown, blue, and gray construction paper. Make one checkered cap. As you read *Caps for Sale*, have the students act as monkeys. When the peddler goes to sleep, have someone take all

the caps, except the checkered cap, and place them on the students' heads. Continue reading as the monkeys mimic the peddler.

3. Dictionary Quiz

The Hat has many words that the students may not know. Divide the class into groups of four and direct each group to be responsible for locating the definitions of eight words. Each person in the group has to look up at least one word.

Use the lap chalkboards for this quiz competition. Directions for this competition are given on p. 32, no. 5.

Write the following words on the board: prickles, hedgehog, gander, gizzard, brambles, snorted, yelped, cozy.

Sample Questions

What word from the word list is the missing word?

1. That is a _____ place to read a book. (*cozy*)

2. The dog _____ at the stranger. (*yelped*)

3. Be careful of _____ on the plants. (*prickles*)

4. The _____ helped the goose make the nest. (*gander*)

5. The bull _____ at the barking dog. (*snorted*)

6. My grandmother uses the _____ of the turkey in her dressing. (*gizzard*)

7. The _____ looks like a porcupine. (*hedgehog*)

8. Blackberries and raspberries are _____ because they have prickly stems. (*brambles*)

4. Hat Day

Sponsor a hat day. Students may wear any kind of hat for the entire day. Encourage them to be creative and decorate their hats. For the privilege of wearing a hat that day, have them donate 25¢ to a cause decided on by the class. They may want to give the money to the American Red Cross, United Way, or to a children's hospital to buy a book.

5. Story Behind a Hat

Have students borrow a hat from a relative and share that hat along with an anecdote about the hat with the class. Use this activity to follow-up *Aunt Flossie's Hats (and Crab Cakes Later)*.

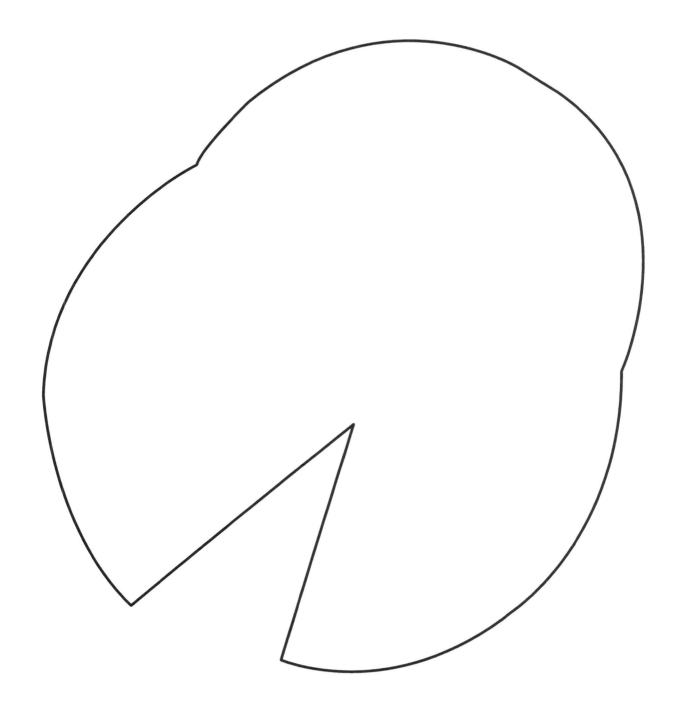

6. Who Took the Teacher's Cap?

Follow-up *Who Took the Farmer's Hat* with a tag game to be played outdoors or in the gymnasium. Have students form a large circle and have them stand with their hands behind their backs with their palms up. Give one student a cap and have her walk around the outside of the circle. The student hands the cap to one of the students in the circle and takes off running around the circle. The student who receives the cap chases. If the first student reaches the spot of her pursuer, that person is declared safe. The student with the cap continues with the same procedure. If the student is tagged, the student gives the hat to another student.

7. Paper Hat

Have students make paper hats out of newspapers. Take a double-spread page of a newspaper and fold it in the shape of a triangle. Cut the large triangle. When unfolded it should be a large square. Cut one for each student. Follow the directions for a paper pocket (see p. 22).

Grade Appropriate Skills Index

	Pre K	K	1	2	3	Language Arts	Science	Mathematics	Art	Social Studies	Library Skills	Page
BEARY FUNNY THINGS TO DO												
Tell Me		✔	✔	✔	✔	✔	✔					18
Bear Rubbing	✔	✔	✔	✔	✔			✔	✔	✔		18
Locating Information on Bears			✔	✔	✔		✔			✔	✔	18
Brown Bear, Brown Bear	✔	✔	✔	✔		✔						18
Comparing Characters		✔	✔	✔	✔	✔						18
Fish for the Bears		✔	✔	✔		✔	✔					21
Pocket for Corduroy		✔	✔	✔	✔	✔				✔		21
Stuffed Bear	✔	✔	✔	✔	✔	✔				✔		23
Sponge Bear/ Number Book	✔	✔	✔	✔	✔					✔		23
Bear Contest	✔	✔	✔	✔	✔					✔		23
Pop-Up Bear		✔	✔	✔	✔	✔						25
Big, Bigger, Biggest		✔	✔	✔				✔				25
Bear Puppet	✔	✔	✔	✔	✔	✔				✔		29
My Favorite Bear Story	✔	✔	✔	✔	✔			✔				29
Bear Day	✔	✔	✔	✔	✔	✔						29
FISH FUNTASY												
Fun With Goldfish		✔	✔					✔				33
Swimmy and Friends	✔	✔	✔			✔						33
Class Book	✔	✔	✔	✔	✔	✔			✔			33
Class Pool		✔	✔	✔	✔	✔			✔			33
Lap Chalkboard Quiz		✔	✔	✔	✔		✔				✔	33
Sea Puzzle		✔	✔	✔			✔		✔			35
Fishing for Words		✔	✔	✔	✔	✔	✔				✔	35
Rainbow Fish	✔	✔	✔	✔	✔	✔			✔			36
Three-Dimensional Fish		✔	✔	✔	✔	✔			✔			39
Fish Mobile	✔	✔	✔	✔					✔			39
Fish Treat	✔	✔	✔	✔	✔	✔	✔	✔				41
Sea Animals – Sources of Information				✔	✔	✔	✔				✔	41
I Was There		✔	✔	✔	✔	✔	✔			✔		41
LITTLE CRITTER BOOKS												
Inch by Inch	✔	✔	✔			✔		✔				44
Who's Missing?		✔	✔	✔	✔	✔		✔				44
Who Is Grouchy?	✔	✔				✔						44
The Very Awesome Caterpillar		✔	✔	✔	✔	✔					✔	44
Critter Hunt			✔	✔	✔	✔	✔					46
Parts of an Insect		✔	✔	✔	✔		✔				✔	46
Parts of an Insect – Songs		✔	✔	✔	✔		✔					46
Caterpillar Treat	✔	✔	✔	✔	✔	✔	✔		✔			48
Buggy Thumbprints	✔	✔	✔	✔	✔		✔		✔			48
Praying Mantis Tag	✔	✔	✔	✔	✔							48
Bookworm Pal		✔	✔	✔	✔				✔			48
Pop-Up Butterfly		✔	✔	✔	✔	✔						49
Bug Olympics		✔	✔	✔	✔							52
Mealworm Magic	✔	✔	✔	✔	✔		✔					53
Mystery Box	✔	✔	✔	✔	✔	✔	✔					54
Very Hungry Caterpillar – Class Book		✔	✔	✔	✔	✔	✔					54
Bee Story		✔	✔	✔	✔	✔			✔		✔	54
Chalkboard Quiz		✔	✔	✔	✔		✔				✔	56
Spider Book		✔	✔	✔	✔	✔			✔			57
BIG RED BARN		✔	✔	✔		✔	✔		✔		✔	58
FARM ANIMALS	✔	✔	✔	✔	✔	✔	✔					59
TIME FOR TURKEY		✔	✔	✔	✔	✔	✔				✔	61
EGG ROLL												
Egg-Rolling Contest	✔	✔	✔	✔	✔							64

Grade Appropriate Skills Index

	Pre K	K	1	2	3	Language Arts	Science	Mathematics	Art	Social Studies	Library Skills	Page
Egg Trivia		✔	✔	✔	✔	✔	✔				✔	65
Favorite Egg	✔	✔	✔	✔	✔				✔			66
Eggsperiment		✔	✔	✔	✔		✔					66
Eggs in a Basket		✔	✔	✔	✔				✔			66
Green Eggs & Ham	✔	✔	✔	✔	✔	✔						66
Mule Eggs for Sale			✔	✔	✔	✔				✔	✔	66
Story Starter	✔	✔	✔	✔	✔	✔				✔		68
Egg Decorating		✔	✔	✔	✔	✔			✔	✔		68
SOMETHING TO DO ABOUT THE												
WEATHER												
What's the Weather		✔	✔	✔	✔	✔	✔				✔	71
It Looks Like …?	✔	✔	✔	✔	✔				✔			71
Don't Melt the Snowmen!												72
Weather Report				✔	✔	✔	✔					73
Signs of the Seasons		✔	✔	✔			✔		✔			73
Sounds of the Weather	✔	✔	✔	✔	✔	✔	✔					73
Sequence Activity		✔	✔			✔						73
Dictionary Fun				✔	✔	✔					✔	75
Snowman Treat	✔	✔	✔	✔	✔				✔			77
Finger-Painting With Shaving Cream	✔	✔	✔						✔			77
Winter Scene	✔	✔	✔			✔						77
Snow Wash	✔	✔	✔	✔	✔				✔			77
Snowflake		✔	✔	✔	✔				✔			77
Dance Show		✔	✔	✔	✔	✔						77
Mushroom in the Rain		✔	✔			✔	✔		✔		✔	79
Let's Make Rain		✔	✔	✔	✔		✔					79
Blinding Blizzard		✔	✔	✔	✔	✔	✔					79
TERRIBLE TROLLS		✔	✔	✔	✔	✔				✔		81
PROGRAMS FOR PLANTS												
Travelling With Miss Rumphius				✔	✔	✔				✔	✔	83
Make the World Beautiful		✔	✔	✔	✔	✔				✔		83
The Carrot Seed	✔	✔	✔	✔		✔						83
Scatter BINGO – Plants		✔	✔	✔	✔		✔					83
Pumpkin Pie	✔	✔	✔	✔	✔	✔		✔			✔	86
Blueberry Treat	✔	✔	✔	✔		✔						86
What Is It?		✔	✔	✔	✔		✔					86
Chalkboard Quiz – Plants		✔	✔	✔	✔		✔					86
What Is My Favorite Vegetable?	✔	✔	✔	✔		✔	✔					87
Vegetable Soup				✔	✔	✔						87
Book Report		✔	✔	✔	✔	✔					✔	89
Plant Cycle		✔	✔	✔	✔		✔					89
Simple Plant Experiments	✔	✔	✔	✔	✔		✔					89
Plant Booklet		✔	✔	✔	✔	✔	✔					89
Grass Heads	✔	✔	✔	✔	✔		✔		✔			91
AESOP'S FABLES – SKITS												
The Miller, His Son & Their Donkey		✔	✔	✔	✔	✔						92
The Shepherd Boy and the Wolf		✔	✔	✔	✔	✔						94
The Ant and the Grasshopper		✔	✔	✔	✔	✔						96
CAPS & HATS & THINGS…												
Match Game	✔	✔	✔	✔	✔	✔		✔				98
Skit	✔	✔	✔			✔						100
Dictionary Quiz			✔	✔	✔	✔					✔	100
Hat Day	✔	✔	✔	✔	✔				✔	✔		100
Story Behind a Hat	✔	✔	✔	✔	✔	✔				✔		102
Who Took the Teacher's Cap	✔	✔	✔									102
Paper Hat		✔	✔	✔	✔	✔			✔			102